The F.B.I.

The F.B.I.

BY QUENTIN REYNOLDS

WILDSIDE PRESS

TO MY GODCHILD
Stephen Humphrey Bogart

Published by Wildside Press LLC
wildsidepress.com

CONTENTS

FOREWORD

Our happiest hours in the F.B.I. occur when we can meet the thousands of young men and women who visit our headquarters annually. We are always glad to answer their questions and to show them our facilities within the limit of our capacity. We look to the young men and women as the citizens of the future who will have it within their power to make a better and more secure America.

Those who cannot visit Washington and our headquarters will find in this book the answers to the questions most frequently raised. That is why we were glad to give our assistance to Quentin Reynolds when he told us of his desire to devote one of the famous Landmark books to the F.B.I.

This book gives you a picture of our headquarters in Washington, D. C., and of the F.B.I. at work. In reading it you will learn something

◀ John Edgar Hoover, the Director of the Federal Bureau of Investigation, United States Department of Justice.

about the way in which fingerprints are processed through our Identification Division and how our laboratory technicians turn the miracles of science into an aid to law enforcement. You will gain an idea of the manner in which instructors conduct classes for new Agents at our training facilities on the Marine Base at Quantico, Virginia. You will find that arrest problems and learning to shoot various weapons on the Firearms Range are only part of the many things which are required of men who want to become Special Agents of the Federal Bureau of Investigation. In reading this book you will gain an idea of the manner in which recruits are turned into skilled investigators, how fugitives are trapped by fingerprints, and how a crime may be solved in the F.B.I. Laboratory. This is the story of the men and the organization which help to preserve the law in our free land.

I am proud of the some 6,000 men who today wear the badge of the F.B.I. As the years go by and these men retire, others will be employed to take their places. Some of you about to read this book may wish to become Special Agents. If you do, now is the time to begin preparing yourself for this profession. I do not mean that you must go out now and learn to handle a gun or classify fingerprints or preserve evidence. We can teach a new Agent to shoot. We can teach him what he needs to know about fingerprints. We can teach him the importance of the most minute bit of evidence. But there are some things required of the Special Agent of the Federal Bureau of Investigation which cannot be taught; they must be developed from childhood. They are the qualities that are embodied in our motto—Fidelity, Bravery, Integrity.

When a young man files an application with the F.B.I., we do not ask if he was the smartest boy in his class. We want to know if he was truthful, dependable, and if he played the game fair. We want to know if he respects his parents, reveres God, honors his flag and loves his country. We can teach the new recruit many things, but we must have a substantial individual to begin with in order to make a G-man.

Every Agent of the Federal Bureau of Investigation has a goal in life—to protect and serve our country. Because we thought it would be a good thing for the boys of America to learn how we strive to completely discharge our responsibilities to our country, it was a pleasure to co-operate in bringing you this account of the F.B.I.

JOHN EDGAR HOOVER
Director, Federal Bureau of Investigation
United States Department of Justice

The F.B.I.

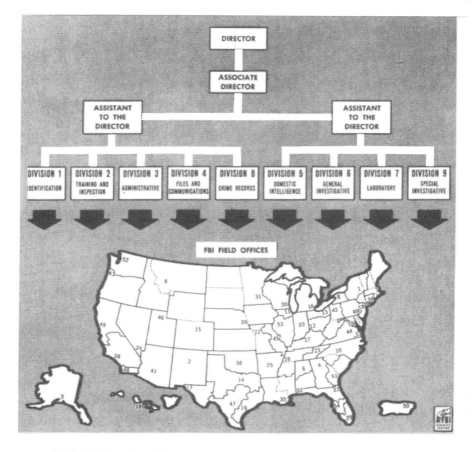

ORGANIZATION OF THE F.B.I.

1 Albany	15 Denver	29 Miami	43 Portland
2 Albuquerque	16 Detroit	30 Milwaukee	44 Richmond
3 Anchorage	17 El Paso	31 Minneapolis	45 St. Louis
4 Atlanta	18 Honolulu	32 Mobile	46 Salt Lake City
5 Baltimore	19 Houston	33 Newark	47 San Antonio
6 Birmingham	20 Indianapolis	34 New Haven	48 San Diego
7 Boston	21 Jacksonville	35 New Orleans	49 San Francisco
8 Buffalo	22 Kansas City	36 New York	50 San Juan, P. R.
9 Butte	23 Knoxville	37 Norfolk	51 Savannah
10 Charlotte	24 Las Vegas	38 Oklahoma City	52 Seattle
11 Chicago	25 Little Rock	39 Omaha	53 Springfield
12 Cincinnati	26 Los Angeles	40 Philadelphia	54 Tampa
13 Cleveland	27 Louisville	41 Phoenix	55 Washington, D. C.
14 Dallas	28 Memphis	42 Pittsburgh	

1 THE BEGINNING AND FUNCTIONS OF THE F.B.I.

"Wanted by the F.B.I."

To the enemy agent, the kidnaper, or the bank robber, these are the most frightening words in the world. Hearing them, the criminal knows that 6,000 F.B.I. agents under the leadership of the greatest man-hunter alive, J. Edgar Hoover, are after him.

But why should the hunted lawbreaker be afraid? America is a big country. There are hundreds of cities and thousands of villages where he can hide. There are big forests and large, uninhabited deserts in the West where he can lose himself. If his crime has been robbery, escape should be especially easy, for the stolen money has made him rich.

"Money can buy anything," he and his fellow criminals boast. With this money he can find a dishonest doctor and have his face completely changed. He can dye his hair and grow a beard so that not even his mother would know him. Why then does he tremble when he hears that he is "Wanted by the F.B.I."?

He trembles because he knows that although hundreds like him have changed their looks and have hidden in remote places, the F.B.I. has always caught up with them. He remembers what happened to Alvin Karpis, John Dillinger, Baby Face Nelson, Machine Gun Kelly, and the other Public Enemies. All are dead or serving life terms. These men disguised themselves. They had plenty of money and good hideouts. Yet one by one they were found by the men of the F.B.I.

The criminal is desperate when he thinks of the 6,000 men who are pursuing him. He determines to fight it out with these agents whom he calls "G-men." Then he remembers that Dillinger and a hundred others tried to fight it out with them. All are dead, for the G-men can shoot straight.

They're smart, too, these G-men. They know every trick that the criminal knows and many more. If he makes just one mistake they'll get him. That is why the man who has just broken the law can't sleep. He becomes nervous, jumping at every sound in the night. This is the beginning of the end, for when a criminal becomes nervous he is almost certain to make a fatal mistake. And then he's no longer "Wanted by the F.B.I." He's been caught by the F.B.I.

The F.B.I. as we know it was born on May 10, 1924, when J. Edgar Hoover was appointed Director of the then Federal Bureau of Investigation by Attorney General Harlan F. Stone, who later became Chief Justice of the United States.

Up to that time there had been a federal law enforcement agency, but it was not very efficient. The United States needed a federal investigative organization that could go anywhere, crossing state lines in pursuit of criminals who had broken federal laws.

After Attorney General Stone had become aware of the need for such an organization, he set about finding a man to direct it. In the process, his eye fell on a lawyer in his own department who had been doing fine work. This was a young man who had received his early schooling in Washington, D.C. At Central High School his agility had earned him the nickname "Speed" among his classmates. "Speed" had gone on to law school, become a lawyer, and then had gone to work for the Department of Justice. His name was John Edgar Hoover.

The Attorney General called twenty-nine-year-old J. Edgar Hoover into his office, and to the young man's amazement announced the plan for a Federal Bureau of Investigation.

"You see," said the Attorney General, "criminals are getting smarter. Today they use stolen automobiles and even airplanes to make their getaways. They have learned to open any lock. The forgers among them can imitate any signature in the world. Even though we're at peace, enemy agents in this country are gathering information to use against us if there should be another war. Their messages to their home countries are written in complicated codes and disappearing ink. The criminal world has discovered science. The old-time law enforcement officer can't beat them because he wasn't trained to fight scientific criminals."

The Attorney General paused and looked gravely at the young man. "I know your record, Edgar," he went on. "You're clever. You're a lawyer. I want you to learn everything there is to know about fingerprinting, handwriting, photography, disappearing ink, and secret codes. When you've learned everything that Scotland Yard and the other police forces of the world can teach you, go out and collect a group of young men like yourself. Open a school and use your training to teach them to be scientific officers. Of course, they must learn to shoot and fight. They should learn jujitsu, too. You'll be the complete boss of the Bureau."

J. Edgar Hoover was careful how he picked his men. To begin with, he insisted that they be between the ages of twenty-five and thirty-five. They had to have a college degree and, in addition, a law degree or a degree in accounting. Old-time policemen sneered at young Hoover and his college boys. "The only law we need," they said, "is the law in the end of a nightstick."

Mr. Hoover didn't agree, so he quietly went ahead with his plans. He investigated every man who applied for a job. He interviewed their friends and their high-school teachers. Sometimes their ministers, their priests, and their rabbis were questioned, for Mr. Hoover would take only men of good character. When it became known that he wanted only "gentlemen" in his department, the old-timers roared with laughter.

Unfortunately they didn't understand what he meant when he used the word "gentleman." He knew that his agents would have to meet all kinds of people. He knew they would have to rub elbows with cultured people as well as with the dregs of society. Mr. Hoover wanted men who could handle a teacup as well as a Tommy gun. He made the F.B.I. the hardest service in the world to get into.

One of the first things done by Mr. Hoover was the establishment of an Identification Division. If the F.B.I. caught a suspect in the old days, his fingerprints were taken immediately. They were then sent around the country and hundreds of local police chiefs were asked if they had any prints which matched them.

Of course this process took weeks. To speed it up Mr. Hoover wanted to have fingerprints of all known criminals housed in a central identification division. Therefore, the 810,188 fingerprint cards on file at Leavenworth Penitentiary and those in the possession of the International Association of Chiefs of Police were consolidated in the F.B.I.'s Identification Division in 1924. At that time, a

A small portion of the Fingerprint Classification Unit in the F.B.I. Identification Division, Washington, D.C.

A fingerprint expert is shown verifying an identification in the Assembly Section of the F.B.I. Identification Division, Washington, D.C.

force of 25 men worked in the Division. Today, there are more than 163 million fingerprint cards on file, and 2,000 employees work in the separate building which houses the cards.

Under J. Edgar Hoover the F.B.I. soon became a strong, intelligent investigative force. Its laboratory became famous all over the country, and police chiefs soon began to realize that the F.B.I. was there to help them. Many small towns are unable to allot much money to police work. As a result, a police chief in such a community cannot afford a laboratory. More than likely, he has not been educated in scientific detective work. His town cannot buy the expensive cameras, microscopes, and instruments needed to identify bits of evidence. When the police chiefs of the country learned that the F.B.I. could assist them in their problems, they called upon it for help in ever-increasing numbers.

Sometimes Mr. Hoover would have to telegraph back sadly, "Sorry, but this isn't in our department." The F.B.I. has the authority to investigate only certain crimes against the federal government.

If a prisoner escapes from a federal prison, it is

the job of the F.B.I. to find him. In most cases, if a person bribes a federal official, the F.B.I. is asked to solve the crime.

Suppose there is a murder on a ship a thousand miles from land? If it is an American ship, the F.B.I. is handed the job of solving the murder. If there is a mutiny, that, too, becomes a problem for the F.B.I. Crimes committed on Indian reservations are assigned to the F.B.I.

These are just a few of the crimes which the F.B.I. was empowered to investigate. There are over 165 federal matters in the F.B.I.'s jurisdiction, but the duty of solving all other crimes rests with local police forces, state troopers, or other federal agencies.

When Congress passed the Federal Bank Robbery Act, it gave the F.B.I. the authority to go after the bank robbers who were terrorizing the nation. Another act of Congress, the National Stolen Property Act, makes it a federal crime to take forged securities or stolen property valued at $5,000 or more from one state to another. Still another act passed by Congress gave the F.B.I. the authority to pursue and capture wanted criminals who had fled from one state to another.

J. Edgar Hoover has always been a strong believer in the rights of local and state police. He does not believe that the F.B.I. should interfere in purely local police problems. However, when a state or a city or a village finds that it must have help from the federal government in Washington, the F.B.I. gives the necessary assistance—*if* it has the authority to do so. For remember, the F.B.I. is governed by certain laws passed by Congress.

The director of the F.B.I. is accountable to the Attorney General of the United States, who presides over the Department of Justice of which the F.B.I. is a part. When the G-men investigate a crime and gather evidence against a suspect, they turn this evidence over to the Attorney General or to one of his representatives, who are called United States attorneys. It is then up to the federal prosecutors to go into court and try the case against the suspect.

2

George "Machine Gun" Kelly was one of those who trembled when he heard that F.B.I. agents, or "Feds," as most criminals called them, were on his trail. He was wanted for kidnaping—one of the crimes most hated by J. Edgar Hoover and every one of his agents.

After pursuing Machine Gun Kelly all over the country, the F.B.I. finally caught up with him in a house in Memphis, Tennessee. Accompanied by the local police, the agents ordered Kelly to surrender. "If you don't, we'll come in for you," one of them called grimly.

There was no answer from inside, and two agents and one police officer with guns in their hands walked into the house. Kelly stood trembling in a corner of the room. He was brave only when he could point his machine gun at unarmed people. It was different now. He raised his hands above his head and whimpered, "Don't shoot, G-men! Don't shoot!"

They didn't shoot, for they hate to waste bullets on cowardly rats like Kelly. As they put handcuffs on him and took him away, one of the agents asked. "What's that you called us, Kelly?"

"G-men," Kelly replied. "You fellows are government men, aren't you? So I call you G-men for short."

That was 'way back in 1933, but the name stuck, although the G-men never apply it to themselves. They prefer the term "agents." But the newspapers and the criminals and the public called them G-men, and gradually they got used to it.

Who are the G-men? Nobody knows. What do they look like? Nobody knows. Of course J. Edgar Hoover and his Associate Director, Clyde Tolson, are known to the public. So are John P. Mohr and Alan H. Belmont, assistants to the Director, and Assistant Directors C. L. Trotter, Alex Rosen, John F. Malone, N. P. Callahan, William S. Tavel, C. D. DeLoach, William C. Sullivan, I. W. Conrad and C. A. Evens. But very few people know the names of the 6,000 agents who are out in the field. They work in secrecy.

How would you like to be a G-man? J. Edgar Hoover is always looking for bright young men to join his department. If you want to be a G-man you have to start early. When Mr. Hoover considers a man, he goes 'way back to his records and behavior at school. His experience tells him that ninety-nine times out of a hundred a decent, healthy boy with a fairly good school record will grow up into a decent, healthy adult.

An agent whom we shall call J—— S—— was such a boy; he grew into such a man. He's a real person, all right. I've met him and he has told me his story.

In the files that Mr. Hoover keeps on every one of his agents it is shown that J—— S—— has had a long record of good work. He has been shot at fifty times. He has been captured by criminals' gangs and has managed to escape each time. He has been successful largely because he has been able to outthink the kidnapers and bank robbers and enemy agents. And when Mr. Hoover talks about him, he says with pride, "Above all, J—— is a good team man."

The F.B.I. operates like a good football team. J. Edgar Hoover is the coach. He picks the players and makes up the plays. When a case "breaks" (to use the language of the G-men), he picks a team and sends it out into the field. He selects one agent who acts as quarterback. This agent calls the signals and the rest of the team obeys perfectly, for G-men never think of individual credit. Their only worry is whether or not their team can beat the gangster team. When it's all over, Mr. Hoover knows which agents did the best teamwork, and they're the ones who are promoted. J—— S—— became a perfect team man.

J—— S—— was born on a little farm in Minnesota. He and his father lived alone, for J——'s mother had died when he was very young.

Then during J——'s junior year at college, his father died and the young man was left alone in the world. When the farm was sold, there was just about enough money to pay all his father's debts. That didn't worry J——; he had worked his way through his first three years at college, so he was no stranger to providing for himself. By doing such odd jobs as waiting on table and fixing furnaces in the winter, he was finally graduated. His marks were only average.

Then he decided to enter law school. He discovered that it was much harder to work his way through law school than it had been to work his way through college. He had only four hours of classroom work each day, but he was expected to do at least another six hours of homework. During his last year he studied criminal law. J—— found this fascinating. He studied the trials of robbers and kidnapers and murderers, and during one of his lectures he heard the professor speak of the F.B.I. as "the greatest law enforcement agency in the world."

"I went through the F.B.I. headquarters in Washington not long ago," the professor said, "and I was greatly impressed by the organization's amazing scientific laboratories. The chemical laboratory is greater than the one we have here at the University of Minnesota. I was also impressed with the F.B.I.'s crime-detecting aids, some of which are so secret that the F.B.I. can't tell you about them. But most of all I was impressed with the men who work under J. Edgar Hoover. In each one of them the words of the F.B.I. motto, 'Fidelity, Bravery, Integrity,' seem to have come to life."

J—— thought about what the professor had said. Then, during his last week at law school, he made up his mind. He wrote to J. Edgar Hoover in Washington saying that he wanted to join the F.B.I. Within a few days he received a letter telling him to report to the Minneapolis office.

The Special Agent in Charge who interviewed him was a friendly, smiling man who had a gift for putting people at their ease. "Tell me something about yourself," he said.

"Well, I was born on a farm. . . ." J—— began.

"So was I," and the Special Agent smiled. "Where was your farm?"

J—— soon found himself talking about his boyhood and his college days.

"My marks were only average," he added a little doubtfully.

"You had to work your way through college," the Special Agent said thoughtfully. "Naturally you had less time than the other students for study."

Then J—— told of his struggle to go through

law school, and of the professor who had spoken about the F.B.I.

"I don't know if I'd be any good," J—— said, "but I wish you would give me a chance."

The Special Agent in Charge told the young man to forget everything he had ever read about the F.B.I. He said that it wasn't always exciting work. G-men, he said, spent most of their time interviewing witnesses, collecting evidence, working in laboratories, checking bank accounts. Sometimes, he admitted, it was dangerous work. And it was always secret work.

"Remember, too," the Special Agent added, "that you will work long hours. Frequently you will be away from your home and family."

"I have no family," J—— said simply.

"You're young now." The Special Agent smiled. "You'll have a family someday."

"Maybe," J—— said, "but all I know is that I'd rather work for the F.B.I. than do anything else in the world."

The Special Agent was impressed. "That's how we all feel," he said. He immediately gave J—— an aptitude test. When a trained examiner reads the answers to the questions asked in such a test, he can form an intelligent opinion as to the kind of work the applicant is best fitted to do. The Special Agent was satisfied that J—— S—— seemed to be the kind of man the F.B.I. wanted, although he didn't tell that to J——.

"There is something I'd like you to do," the Special Agent said casually to J—— that afternoon. "A young man named Roddy Farmer has made application to join the F.B.I. We don't know much about him, but he gave a reference—a man named William Kirk, who is registered at the Statler Hotel. I'd like you to call on Kirk and learn everything he knows about Roddy Farmer."

J—— S—— hurried to the Statler. He found William Kirk to be a smiling, pleasant man who said that he had known the applicant all his life. "Farmer is not only a good, smart young fellow," Kirk said earnestly, "but he was a great athlete at Duke University. In his senior year he was captain of the Duke team and was named on *Collier's* All-American team."

"May I ask what your business is, Mr. Kirk?" J—— asked politely.

"Of course," and Kirk smiled. "I am vice-president of the Terminal Cab Company in New York City. I live at 829 Park Avenue. I'm a member of the University Club and the New York Athletic Club. I tell you, this young Roddy Farmer will be a great asset to the F.B.I., and if I were you I would recommend him highly to your superiors."

J—— S—— said good-bye and went down into the hotel lobby. William Kirk certainly seemed like a fine man, and if he vouched for Roddy Farmer, the applicant must be worthy.

But J—— S—— was not only cautious, he was also bright. It came to him suddenly that he knew nothing about William Kirk except what Kirk had told him.

He reported to the Special Agent in Charge who had given him the assignment.

"I'll give you a stenographer," the Agent said. "You dictate your report to her. Just put it in your own words, and if you have any suggestions, don't hesitate to make them."

J—— was left alone in a small office with a stenographer. What should he say? Should he say that the applicant Roddy Farmer was okay in every way? But how did he know Roddy Farmer *was* okay? What about William Kirk? Suppose he had been lying? J—— drew a deep breath and started to dictate.

"I talked to William Kirk and questioned him about the applicant Roddy Farmer. He recommended him highly. Kirk says he is a vice-president of the Terminal Cab Company in New York. I have only his word for that. Mr. Kirk says that the applicant Roddy Farmer graduated from Duke University and was named on *Collier's* All-American team. I would check with Duke University and then with *Collier's* to see if these facts are true."

The stenographer typed out the report and then gave it to the Special Agent. He called J—— into his office. J—— was pretty nervous. After all, William Kirk might be everything he claimed to be, in which case he, J——, would feel foolish about having cast suspicion on him. But the Agent had said, "If you have any suggestions, don't hesitate to make them." Well, he had had suggestions to make and he'd made them!

He stood in front of the Special Agent who was reading the report.

"You seem suspicious of William Kirk," the Special Agent said, looking up at him.

"Not suspicious," J—— said earnestly. "But I

have only his word for it that he's vice-president of the Terminal Cab Company."

"Why didn't you ask him for some cards or credentials to show who he was?"

"I thought of that," J—— said. "But then I realized that if he was a fake, he'd have fake cards."

The Special Agent laughed. "As a matter of fact, William Kirk is not a phony."

"He isn't?" J——'s jaw dropped.

"No, he's one of our most experienced agents! This was just one more test for you."

J—— just blinked, too relieved to say anything.

"Now it's time you had a physical examination," the Special Agent said.

J—— was sent to another room where a doctor was waiting. He had to answer a great many questions as to what sicknesses he had ever had. The doctor gave him every possible test. He was very particular about the eye test. F.B.I. agents have to have just about perfect eyesight, and they have to have quick reflexes. They undergo about the same kind of physical examination as applicants for the Air Force. When the examination was over, J—— returned to the Special Agent in Charge.

"You'll hear from us," the Special Agent said,

but J—— couldn't tell from his voice whether he had passed or not.

Now came the hardest part of all—the waiting.

J—— had no idea whether he had passed the first tests or not. Thinking it over, he felt that he'd been too particular about William Kirk. He decided that he'd paid too much attention to Kirk and hadn't asked enough questions about Farmer. That's just about what the Special Agent in Charge had decided too, but he put it down to J——'s inexperience. The young man was certainly willing, he felt, and alert.

Meanwhile other agents were investigating J——'s whole life. Within a month they knew everything there was to be known about him. There are two things to which the F.B.I. pays special attention when considering an applicant—character and fitness. J——'s test showed that he qualified on the score of fitness, but what about character?

J. Edgar Hoover has always believed that a man's character is formed as a boy. If a boy cheats in school, the chances are a hundred to one that he'll cheat in later life, and the F.B.I. has no place for cheaters. J——'s early teachers were interviewed. They were frank and honest with the Special Agent who interviewed them.

"As a kid, young J—— liked hunting and fishing much more than he did studying," one of them said.

"What kid doesn't?" The agent grinned. He didn't hold this against J——. He'd been a farm boy himself.

Had J—— ever cheated? Had he ever lied? Had he ever been a bully? The teachers all answered "No" to these questions.

"J—— was just a normal boy," one of them said. "He was decent, fun-loving, and he loved his father very much. He was a boy you could trust."

"That's what we want," the agent said. "Men we can trust."

Then the Special Agent interviewed J——'s college professors and the dean of the college. He talked to J——'s law professors and to the boys who had gone to college and law school with J——. He talked to the landlady in the rooming house where J—— had lived, and then he forwarded all his reports to Washington.

One day J—— received a notice to report to the F.B.I. office in Minneapolis. He was interviewed by another Special Agent who had J——'s record in front of him.

"I've been looking over your record, J——," the agent said. "When you talked to our Special Agent before, you left out quite a bit."

"I didn't mean to," J—— said, alarmed.

"You never told our representative that you were a Boy Scout leader," the agent said.

"Gosh, that was so long ago I'd forgotten it," J—— explained.

"You never told us either that your uncle had been a congressman and that he was now a judge."

"I didn't think that was important," J—— said a bit nervously.

"It isn't important." The F.B.I. man laughed. "Political influence doesn't mean a thing to Mr. Hoover or to our department. We just do our job without any outside interference. I will say your teachers and your father's friends think a lot of you."

"I'm glad to know that," J—— said fervently.

"We've decided to consider your application," the F.B.I. man went on. "Of course, you have a long way to go yet before you're accepted, but at least your character is good."

A week later J—— S—— received a telegram telling him to report to the F.B.I. headquarters in Washington, D. C. His application had been accepted. It was the happiest day of his life.

A view of the United States Department of Justice Building, Washington, D. C., which houses the Federal Bureau of Investigation.

3 THE F.B.I. TRAINING COURSE

When J—— S—— reported to Washington, he found that he was one of forty-five young men who had successfully passed the tests. The Assistant Director who was to swear them in announced that 875 men had applied for entrance to the F.B.I. All had been tested thoroughly, but of the 875 only these forty-five had been accepted. Then, as the Assistant Director recited the words of the oath of office, the young men repeated them after him:

> . . . I do solemnly swear that I will support and defend the Constitution of the United States against all enemies, foreign and domestic; that I will bear true faith and allegiance to the same; that I take this obligation freely, without any mental reservation or purpose of evasion; and that I will well and faithfully discharge

the duties of the office on which I am about to enter, so help me God.

"You have been sworn in now," the Assistant Director told the forty-five happy young men. "But for the next year you will be on probation. Your training course will be a hard one; the passing grade is 85 per cent. Anyone who drops below that will immediately be sent home. Tonight you will be taken to the F.B.I. Academy at Quantico, Virginia, to begin fourteen weeks of intensive training. Your classes will begin at nine and end at six, and you will have plenty of homework. In this course we separate the men from the boys. But there is no reason why all of you shouldn't pass if you work hard."

That night J—— and the other young G-men climbed into a bus and were driven to Quantico, which is about thirty-eight miles from Washington. The bus stopped in front of a large building where the young men were to live. There were four cots to a room and a locker for each man. The trainees would make their own beds and keep their rooms clean. On the ground floor there was

F.B.I. Academy located on the Marine Base, Quantico, Virginia.

a large dining room and a recreation room. There were also several large classrooms.

The next morning the training course began. There were courses in more than a hundred subjects dealing with the various phases of law enforcement, including scientific crime detection, fingerprinting, interviewing witnesses and suspects, searching of crime scenes, federal criminal procedure, and the Constitution and Bill of Rights. In addition to this, the men spent an hour a day learning jujitsu and the way to disarm a man who is pointing a gun at you.

Then came the day when they were brought to the firing range. They had to become expert with the .38-caliber police revolver, the .30-caliber rifle, the .45-caliber submachine gun, the 12-gauge shotgun. They had to learn to handle the powerful .357-caliber magnum revolver.

J—— found that the instructor in shooting was Special Agent Henry Sloan, called "Hank" by his fellow agents. A tall, lean, smiling man, "Hank" Sloan asked how many of the new men had never fired a gun before. About fifteen of them raised their hands.

Special Agents of the F.B.I. receiving training in firing a Thompson sub-machine gun on the F.B.I. Range, Quantico, Virginia.

Special Agents engaging in hip shooting practice on one of the firearms ranges of the F.B.I. Academy, Quantico, Virginia.

"You'll probably end up being the best shots in this class." Sloan grinned. "You haven't acquired any bad shooting habits. You're starting from scratch, and you'll be easier to teach."

Long afterward J—— remembered "Hank" Sloan as the most patient instructor he'd ever had. "Hank" never lost his temper; he was always genial and friendly. Other instructors told the new men that "Hank" was one of the ten best marksmen in the country.

J—— enjoyed this part of the training. His shooting with the rifle and the shotgun earned him approving smiles from the instructors. He didn't do so well with the revolver. In fact, none of the new agents was very skillful with this weapon.

"A revolver is good only for short-range shooting," their instructor said. "Forget everything you've ever seen in western movies. Those old-time bandits who were supposed to be so quick on the draw were rank amateurs. Within a month you'll be able to do things with a gun none of them ever dreamed about. Comparatively few men can hit anything with a revolver at more than thirty feet. You'll be able to hit a target every time at sixty yards."

A class of Special Agents receives instructions in disarming methods on the roof gymnasium, F.B.I. Academy, Quantico, Virginia.

A Special Agent of the F.B.I. firing from a sitting position on the Practical Pistol Course at the F.B.I. Academy, Quantico, Virginia.

Day after day J—— practiced with the revolver. At first he had to fire ten shots from the hip at a distance of seven yards. He had to reload after his first five shots and get all ten shots off in twenty-five seconds. Also, he had to hit the target every time.

"You are not a good shot," Sloan said, "until you can draw your gun, fire, and reload without thinking about what you are doing."

Finally, after a month of this, the instructors told J—— that they were satisfied with his shooting.

"Now we will start all over," the chief instructor said casually. "But this time you will hold the gun in your left hand."

"I can't do that," J—— said falteringly. "I'm not left-handed."

"You will be before long," and the instructor laughed.

He was right. It was very hard to learn to shoot well with the left hand, but it was absolutely necessary. A man who can shoot equally well with either hand has a tremendous advantage over the average criminal, who can shoot only with his right hand.

"If your right hand is hit," the instructor pointed

out, "you can switch the gun to your left hand and keep on firing. And you have to be good at it. Remember, when a G-man fires he shoots to kill. Your hardest job—and only experience can teach you this—is to know when to fire. Never fire unless you, another agent, or an innocent bystander is in danger of being killed by the criminal you are trying to capture."

J—— not only had to learn to shoot with both hands; he also had to learn to strip down his guns, clean them, and reassemble them while blindfolded.

"Gangsters often use Tommy guns," J—— was told. His instructor added that gangsters seldom take good care of their weapons, and often their Tommy guns jam. J—— was taught how to keep his Tommy gun from jamming.

Records were kept of the hits made by the young agent. The target was the life-size figure of a man reaching for his gun. Every time a student hit this figure in a spot that would kill him, he received two points. It was a big day for J—— when, after taking fifty shots at the target, the instructor announced that his score was one hundred. He was the first of the class to achieve the perfect score, and that night during dinner the chief instructor presented him with a small gold medal for expert marksmanship.

Not all of the instruction was done at Quantico. Now and then a group was taken into Washington to study at the laboratories in the main building. At other times they were taught the important subject of identification at the F.B.I.'s Identification Building.

J— S— found out that each day the F.B.I. receives about 23,000 sets of fingerprints for processing. Some of these are sent to the F.B.I.'s Identification Division by local and state police and by law enforcement agencies in friendly foreign countries. Usually the fingerprint cards sent by police contain the finger impressions of persons who have just been arrested, and the police want to know if the F.B.I. can verify their identity and whether the files show a record of previous arrests. Within two days after receipt, the answers to these questions are sent.

J— S— learned everything there was to be learned about the ways to identify a man. Many criminals have operations on their fingertips in an effort to escape identification. Or they mutilate

Training School of Special Agents of the Federal Bureau of Investigation, United States Department of Justice.

their fingertips so that no prints can be taken. But what they usually forget is that the middle parts of the fingers show prints as well as the tips.

During the sessions at the laboratory J—— learned to identify a bullet dug out of a murdered man. He was taught how various instruments can be used to show whether a certain bullet has come from the gun of a suspect. He learned it is possible to analyze a minute particle of paint and help determine the year and make of the automobile from which it came. He was taught that sometimes it is possible, after studying a lipstick stain on a woman's handkerchief, to find out the trade name of the lipstick as well as the name of the manufacturer.

J—— acquired a great respect for the scientists in the various laboratories in the big F.B.I. building. These men are great scientists, and a number of them hold doctors' degrees. They taught J—— that animal blood can be differentiated from human blood. They taught him to be alert in examining documents and to consider the possibility of invisible writing and forgeries. They showed him how they could tell whether a tiny piece of hair came from a human being or from an animal. They taught him a thousand and one other things.

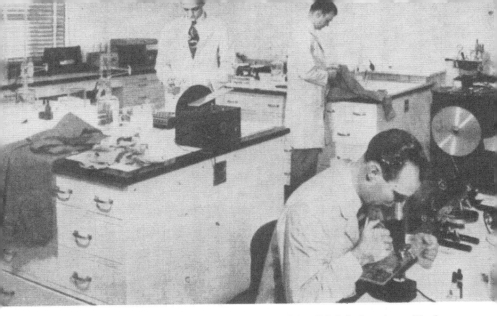

A general view of the Serological Section of the F.B.I. Laboratory, Washington, D.C.

A technician in the F.B.I. Laboratory, Washington, D.C., developing latent fingerprints on an extortion note with iodine fumes.

At the end of fourteen weeks J—— S—— had passed all his tests with a mark of 95. Now at last he was a full-fledged G-man, for he had already been given his badge, a brief case, a .38-caliber Colt, and his identification card.

Young agents are transferred from one field office to another. J—— S—— was stationed in Boston for a year, in San Francisco for a year, and he spent another year in small southern towns. Every four years he is summoned back to Washington for two weeks. So is every other agent in the F.B.I. During that time they practice their shooting and are brought up to date on scientific means of detecting crime, for the F.B.I. has to keep one step ahead of the criminals who are devising new methods of extorting money, burglarizing safes, and committing other unlawful acts.

4   F.B.I. FIELD OFFICE ASSIGNMENT

Following orders, J—— S—— reported to the Boston office. His superior there was a veteran of the Federal Bureau of Investigation.

"You have learned a lot during the past fourteen weeks," said the veteran agent with a smile, "and now you can start putting some of that learning to use. For the next few months your work will be chiefly routine. You'll find a great deal of it dull, but experience is the best teacher in the world, and that's what you need now—experience."

For the next few days J—— accompanied an experienced Special Agent on his rounds. He sat quietly while the Special Agent interviewed suspects, businessmen, and police chiefs. Then one day the older agent said casually, "From now on you do the interviewing and I'll sit by quietly."

Gradually J—— became expert at interviewing people. He found that there was a certain knack to questioning, and that if a man had that knack, people talked to him freely and often gave him information which they really didn't want to give.

Finally the Special Agent in Charge, or S.A.C., as he is known to his subordinates, sent him out on his own. By now he was accustomed to the routine of the office. No matter where he was (unless it was a special assignment), he phoned his F.B.I. field office every three hours. Every G-man in the country does that. The Special Agent in charge of an office knows at all times just where his men are and how they can be reached. In case of an emergency, he can order them all to report almost immediately.

One day the S.A.C. said to J——, "I want you to investigate something going on in Marion, a little town about a hundred miles west of here. The chief of police has been receiving some threatening letters and he's asked us to help him out."

"Fine," and J—— beamed. It was his first chance to go out in the field and do a job on his own.

"James Furey, the chief of police in Marion, has received four anonymous letters," said the S.A.C. "These notes state that unless he resigns his post as chief of police by Saturday, April 23rd, he will be killed. Each letter was printed and each was signed 'The Glove.' One of the letters also said that if the chief does not resign, three prominent citizens of the town will be killed."

"Isn't this a case for the local police?" J—— asked.

"We entered the case," the Special Agent said, "because the mailing of such threatening letters is a violation of a federal law. That's why Chief of Police Furey has sent the letters to our laboratory in Washington and has asked that we give him help. These letters may be the work of some crank, some schoolboy who has a grudge against the Chief, or some desperate criminal who means what he says. We just can't take a chance. Here are photostatic copies of the letters. The Chief is expecting you, so you'd better get going."

J—— S—— found the Chief greatly worried, for he could think of only one group of men who might have a serious grievance against him. A few years before, there had been a series of robberies in the town. The Chief had captured the criminals and they had been sent to prison. After they were sentenced, they vowed that they would get revenge. Two of them had now been released from jail.

"I doubt very much if they sent these letters,"

Chief Furey told J—— S——, "but I suppose we must consider every possibility. They might well have been written by some high-school kid whom I have reprimanded for a traffic violation or some such thing."

He shook his head, looking puzzled. Then as J—— S—— waited, Chief Furey went on. "We don't have a laboratory here in Marion where the printing of the notes can be analyzed or compared with the writing of possible suspects," he said. "I know that you fellows are expert at that sort of thing and, anyway, this is a federal violation. Since I'd tell the bank president to report the letters to the F.B.I. if he had received them, I certainly want you to take this over."

J—— phoned Washington to ask about the two criminals who had been released from jail. They had been tracked down. Because both were living in California, he ruled them out.

His next step was to ask the Chief of Police for a list of all known local lawbreakers. Marion was a law-abiding town for the most part and only ten or twelve of its citizens had been imprisoned within the preceding few years. Some of these were still in jail. J—— S—— interviewed the others. He soon became convinced that none of them had had anything to do with writing the letters. His reasoning was based on the fact that the letters did not ask for money or for ransom, but merely demanded that the Chief of Police resign his position. Because of this J—— was pretty sure that the notes were the work of someone who had a personal grudge, or someone who was trying to attract notice to himself. The latter theory seemed more likely when J—— S—— found that the Chief was the most popular man in town.

"Nobody hates the Chief," said one man who had just got out of jail. "I stole an automobile and he caught me. I faced a long sentence, but at the trial the Chief said that if the court would give me a light sentence, he'd find a job for me when I'd served my term. I was in a year, and when I got out, the Chief had a job waiting for me in this garage. I've been working here two years, I'm married, I have a kid, and people have forgotten about my one mistake. Thanks to the Chief, I'm now a respected member of the town. No, Mister, if you think someone has a grudge against the Chief, you're barking up the wrong tree."

J—— S—— wondered if the letters could be the

work of an insane person or of some crank. He spoke to the local doctors, and they declared that to their knowledge there wasn't a single person in Marion who had ever been committed to an insane asylum or who seemed in any way to be insane. J—— S—— was a bit discouraged. Then he had a sudden thought. Could the letters possibly be the work of some high-school youngster? He went to the principal of Marion High School and talked with him and with several of the teachers.

"I'm looking for some high-school boy or girl who might be a show-off," he said. "Can you think of any students who will do anything just to be noticed?"

"Well, there's Jimmy Lane," one teacher said thoughtfully. "I must say he loves the limelight."

"That's true," the principal said dryly, "but he gets all the attention he wants without having to write anonymous letters. He's captain of the football team and president of his class."

They mentioned the names of several other students, but when J—— S—— investigated them not a single one seemed the type to threaten the Chief of Police with death. A few days later the principal mentioned a boy named Earnest Shore.

"I have nothing against Ernie," the principal said, "except that he never really fitted into the life of the high school. All his friends are much older than he is, and he never brings a high-school girl to any of our dances. He seems to prefer older girls. I have nothing against him," the principal repeated, "but he is unquestionably a show-off. He's always trying to impress the other students with his importance."

"May I talk to him?" J—— S—— asked.

The principal sent for Earnest Shore, and when the boy arrived, he appeared calm and cool. In fact, he seemed quite pleased at the idea of being questioned by a G-man. He was also a little contemptuous of J—— S——.

"Would you mind printing a note?" the agent asked him. "I'll dictate it to you."

"Sure," and Ernie grinned. "I'll be glad to."

J—— S—— picked up one of the extortion letters and dictated:

> Chief Furey,
>   Warning Number 3.
>   You are marked!
>   Unless you resign your office as chief

of police by Friday, April 22, you will die at 9:00 p.m., on Saturday, April 23. Will you please put in the Marion Daily Eagle, Friday, April 22,—your decision as to whether or not you will resign. If you do not, three prominent citizens will die.

THE GLOVE

When the seventeen-year-old boy had finished, he looked up impudently and asked, "Is that all, G-man?"

"That's all for now," J—— S—— replied quietly.

"Everybody prints letters the same, G-man," Shore said with a smirk. "You ought to know that."

"This is just routine," the agent said. "We've asked a great many people in town to print the letter."

J—— S—— went back to his hotel room and compared the note sent to Chief Furey with the one that Shore had just printed.

As J—— S—— looked at the two notes, he noticed that in each one the formations of certain letters were quite similar. But he knew that among the scientists in the F.B.I. laboratory in Washington were the world's greatest experts in the analysis of handwriting. He immediately mailed Shore's note to the F.B.I. in Washington, and two days later received an answer.

"This sample of Shore's hand printing proves conclusively that it was he who wrote the notes to Chief of Police Furey." The report pointed out that the "f" in the word "Chief" was exactly the same in both notes. So was the "y" in Furey. Shore had a very peculiar way of making a "g." So did the person who had written the threatening letter to Chief Furey. In all, there were ten examples which proved conclusively that the same person had written both notes.

J— S— went at once to Shore's home and confronted him with the evidence. Under the agent's gentle questioning, the boy finally broke down and confessed. He said that he and his girl had written the letters "to create some excitement in Marion." In order to avoid fingerprints, Shore had worn a glove when he wrote the threatening notes. He did not know that every person had an individual way of writing and printing.

J— S— arrested Shore and the girl, who also admitted her part in the writing of the letters. Both

Operating an enlarger in the photographic laboratory of the Federal Bureau of Investigation, U. S. Department of Justice.

insisted they had meant no harm, and that they had never intended to carry out their threat to kill the Chief of Police. The story had started several years before when Earnest Shore's two brothers, both much older than he, had been arrested by Chief of Police Furey for stealing an automobile. The two men carried no grudge against the Chief, but their young brother had felt very bitter about the affair.

Both Shore and the girl were tried, and Shore was sent to a correctional institution where he was to remain until his twenty-first birthday. The girl was sentenced to six months and was then placed on probation. When J—— S—— returned to the Boston field office, he was congratulated by the S.A.C.

"It wasn't a very important case," J—— said.

"Every case is important," the Special Agent in Charge replied gravely. "If those two youngsters had not been found out, they would have thought it possible to get away with anything. As a result, they might now be on their way to leading criminal lives."

"Our laboratory men deserve some of the credit," said J——. "They clinched the case when they assured me that Shore had written the letters."

The S.A.C. laughed. "I can see you learned

something important while you were in Marion," he said. "You learned that when you're out on a case you're never alone. You have the greatest laboratories in the world behind you in Washington. A piece of cloth, a scrap of paper, a speck of dust, a small bloodstain can tell important stories to the men in the F.B.I. Laboratory. Never hesitate to call on them."

5   THE BREMER KIDNAPING CASE

As the fame of the F.B.I. increased, Congress gave it more work to do. In 1932 the little son of Charles A. Lindbergh was kidnaped. The crime shocked the whole world. The kidnaper demanded $50,000 in ransom, and the money was paid. But by that time the little boy was dead.

The country was horrified. So was Congress, which soon passed the Federal Kidnaping Statute, or "The Lindbergh Law," as it is more commonly known. This law states that a kidnaper who takes his victim from one state to another commits a federal offense. The criminal's arrest then becomes the work of the F.B.I.

There had been a wave of kidnapings, but the F.B.I. had been unable to do much about them, and many local police forces had neither the training nor the equipment to track down these vicious criminals. No wonder the policemen of the country were happy with the new law! Now if there was a kidnaping in their territory in violation of the federal law, they had only to phone J. Edgar Hoover. Then within an hour or so a group of trained F.B.I. agents would be on the spot, for Mr. Hoover had organized "field offices" all over the country. J—— S——, for instance, worked out of the Boston office. There are F.B.I. offices in major cities in the country, and each office is in constant communication with Mr. Hoover in his Washington office. From there he supervises the activities of all agents.

J—— S—— learned a great deal just from listening to the older, more experienced agents. They told him of the days of gang warfare in the 1920's and 1930's and of how, for example, they had rounded up the notorious "Ma" Barker gang and put an end to Alvin Karpis, known in those days as Public Enemy Number One.

Alvin Karpis did not steal because he was hungry or because he couldn't get a job. At the age of sixteen he had decided that he would never work for a living, although he was envious of boys whose families had more money than his own. Perhaps his dislike of work came from his hatred of getting up early, even to go to school. He was a sullen, bad-tempered boy who enjoyed reading about the activities of those in the criminal world.

Alvin Karpis lived in Topeka, Kansas. He and the gang of teen-age kids with whom he traveled lived in a poor section of the city where there were no playgrounds or parks. A Y.M.C.A. secretary knew about this gang and he knew, too, that they weren't all vicious or mean. He organized a club for them with a program of activities which were carried on under the guidance of the Y.M.C.A.

"You can play handball and basketball," he said, "and we'll teach you to box. We have a swimming pool, and you'll find you can have a lot more fun at the Y than you can on the streets."

Ten of the eleven boys eagerly accepted the invitation of the secretary of the Y.M.C.A. But not Alvin Karpis. He wasn't going to be a "sissy," he sneered. He became a kind of "lone wolf" while the other boys had fun at the Y. Then Alvin started to break into candy stores and grocery stores and rifle the cash registers. One day he broke into a jewelry shop and got away with several valuable pieces of jewelry.

Karpis tried to sell some of the stolen goods to a respectable pawnbroker, who tipped off the police. As a result, Karpis was caught, tried, and sentenced to ten years in the reformatory. He served only two years and then he escaped. He went to Tulsa, Oklahoma, and in 1931 joined forces with a criminal named Arthur Barker, known as "Doc" Barker, in a career of big-time crime. Assisting them were "Doc" Barker's three brothers and their mother, a fat, pleasant-looking woman. From her appearance no one would ever have suspected that she was one of the trickiest, most evil criminals in the country. "Ma" Barker, as she was known to the world of gangsters, trained all four of her sons to be hoodlums, highwaymen, kidnapers, and murderers.

The lawless activities of "Ma" Barker and her four sons were known to the F.B.I., but they had been unable to get any real evidence against the gang. "Ma" Barker was clever enough to plan crimes that did not break the federal law.

It was to her headquarters at Tulsa, Oklahoma, that her son brought Alvin Karpis, and "Ma" Barker became his teacher in crime. At that time she had twenty hoodlums in her gang. She planned the robberies and the getaways. When a robbery was over, she hid those who took part in it. If any of the criminals were caught, she hired lawyers to defend them. If they escaped from prison, she sheltered them in a hideout in the Cookson Hills of Oklahoma.

"Ma" Barker was drunk with power. She felt that she was above the law. Although the police and the F.B.I. knew that she was responsible for at least a hundred robberies, she had never spent one day of her life in jail. She sneered at sheriffs and police chiefs. She even sneered at the F.B.I. That was her big mistake.

In the meantime, Alvin Karpis had become such an important member of the gang that the other members looked up to him as "Ma" Barker's Number 2 man. Karpis thought that he could get away with anything. What he did after he and "Doc" Barker robbed a store in Missouri is proof of this.

The two gangsters made their getaway in a De-Soto automobile. The next day they left the car in a garage where it was recognized by a mechanic who notified Sheriff C. R. Kelly of White Plains, Missouri. When the brave sheriff walked into the garage to question Karpis and Barker, Karpis and Barker fired at the sheriff and killed him. As a result, police of the entire country were on the hunt for Barker and Karpis. But they kept out of sight in one of "Ma" Barker's hideouts.

Then "Ma" Barker moved her whole gang to St. Paul, Minnesota. She and Alvin Karpis had decided that the easiest way to make big money was to kidnap a wealthy citizen and hold him for ransom.

"That means we'll have to fight the F.B.I.," her son Fred said a little doubtfully.

"Your old mother is smarter than the F.B.I.," "Ma" Barker boasted. "You just leave the thinking to Alvin and me, and obey orders."

"Ma" Barker decided to kidnap Edward George Bremer, whose family was one of the wealthiest in St. Paul. The gang studied Bremer's movements carefully. They knew that every morning he drove his nine-year-old daughter to school. One morning he dropped the little girl in front of the school and then started to drive to his office. Unknown to Bremer, a big black car followed him. Two blocks from the school he stopped for a traffic light. Suddenly a man appeared on the left side of the car, stuck a gun against Bremer's ribs, and said, "Move over."

The gunman opened the door and slid behind

the wheel. At the same moment another of the gang stepped into the car from the other side and hit Bremer on the head with a heavy instrument. He slumped to the floor, unconscious. Then the two gunmen drove off with him.

The next day Walter Magee, a close friend of the Bremer family, received a ransom note. The spelling wasn't very good but the note was clear enough. It read as follows:

> You are hereby declared in on a very desperate undertaking. Dont try to cross us. Your future and B's are the important issue. Follow these instructions to the letter. Police have never helped in such a spot, and wont this time either. You better take care of the payoff first and let them do the detecting later. Because the police usually butt in, your friend isn't none to comfortable now so don't delay the payment. We demand $200,000. Payment must be made in 5 and 10 dollar bills—no new money—no consecutive numbers—large variety of issues. Place the money in two large suit box cartons

big enough to hold the full amount and tie with heavy cord. No contact will be made until you notify us that you are ready to pay as we direct. You place an ad in the Minneapolis Tribune as soon as you have the money ready. Under personal colum (We are ready Alice). You will then receive your final instructions. Be prepared to leave at a minutes notice to make the payoff. Dont attempt to stall or outsmart us. Dont try to bargain. Dont plead poverty we know how much they have in their banks. Dont try to communecate with us we'll do the directing. Threats arent necessary—you just do your part—we guarantee to do ours.

There was a note attached to this in the handwriting of Edward Bremer. It said:

I have named you as payoff man. You are responsible for my safety. I am responsible for the full amount of the money.
(Signed) E. G. Bremer
Deal only when signature is used.

Magee immediately notified the F.B.I. Back in Washington, J. Edgar Hoover held a conference with his chief assistants. The Bremer kidnaping appeared to them to be the work of the "Ma" Barker gang. That meant that Alvin Karpis was mixed up in it. Mr. Hoover sent twenty extra agents to St. Paul.

There they learned that the Bremer family, anxious to save the life of the victim, was ready to pay the ransom. Mr. Hoover, who had taken charge of this case, told the family to go ahead, for he has always insisted that the life of a kidnaping victim has to be protected. Once the ransom money was paid and Edward Bremer returned to safety, Mr. Hoover and his agents would go after the gang.

By this time the kidnapers knew that the G-men were in St. Paul. Another note in the handwriting of Edward Bremer was delivered to his friend, Walter Magee. It read:

Dear Walter,

I am sorry to have called on you, but I felt you were the old standby. Tell the family that I am all right. The people that have me know that the police and G-men are after them. Walter, please call them off and work all alone. The people who have me are going to give you a new plan for the ransom money. Work according to their directions. Again I say, do it alone, no police, just you.

Edward

Meanwhile, Mr. Bremer's automobile had been found. There were bloodstains on the front seat, and some of the newspapers said that the victim was probably dead. Edward Bremer knew that this would be a source of worry to his wife, so he wrote the following letter to her:

Dearest Patz,

Please don't worry. Everything will come out all right. Tell Hertzey to be a good little girl. Her Daddy is thinking of her all the time. All I want is to see you and her again. I suppose you were worrying about the blood in the front seat of the car. I had a cut on my head which bled a lot, but it has been dressed and is all right now. I am treated well and the

only thing I have to ask is to keep the police out of this. Then I will be returned
to you all safely. Yours,

Ed

When Mr. Hoover read this note, he said to his agents, "We don't want to do anything that will make the kidnapers kill Edward Bremer. We'll wait until he is returned."

Now Walter Magee received another note telling him how to deliver the $200,000 in ransom money. He was to drive to Farmington, Minnesota, and proceed to the bus terminal in time for the departure of the bus that left at 9:25 each night. He was to follow this bus until he saw four red lights on the left side of the road. Just beyond the four red lights he was to turn off on the first road to the left and continue until he saw the headlights of a car flash five times. Then he was to stop his car and put the two boxes containing the ransom money on the right side of the road.

Walter Magee did everything that the gang had told him to do. He then drove home. The next day Bremer was released.

As soon as Mr. Hoover knew that Bremer was

safe, he called his agents together for a conference. "Now," he said grimly, "go after these rats."

The first job of the G-men was to find out where Bremer had been hidden. When they questioned the victim, he could give little information for he had been blindfolded most of the time. Then, bit by bit, he recalled facts that seemed unimportant but which were to be of great value to the F.B.I. At night, he said, his blindfold was taken off. For this reason he was able to give Mr. Hoover's men a good description of the bedroom in which he had been locked, and to describe the wallpaper in great detail. Within twelve hours the G-men had samples of all wallpaper sold in St. Paul during the preceding few years. Bremer was able to identify one specimen as being the kind of wallpaper on the bedroom in the hideaway.

The case had gone forward another step, but more facts were needed. "Try to remember every sound that you heard during your captivity, Mr. Bremer," the G-men prompted.

Bremer dug into his memory and came up with the information that there were two dogs outside the hideaway. Although he had never seen them, he had heard them bark quite often. He also remembered that every day he had heard children playing outside the house.

Two or three times a day sounds had come from the next room. It seemed that coal was being shoveled from a bin into a scuttle. Probably the sounds had come from a coal stove in a kitchen.

Now that the flow of recollections had started, Bremer found it easy to go on. He described the noise of the traffic outside the house. He said that quite often he had heard brakes being applied either to buses or trucks. More than likely, this meant that the house was near a STOP sign. He also said that he could hear the sounds of trains and that they seemed fairly close. He did not know, of course, whether the hide-out was in St. Paul or in nearby Rochester, Minnesota, or in some smaller city.

With the help of Bremer's clues, the F.B.I. agents were able to locate the house in which he had been kept, but it was empty. Meanwhile, the observant Bremer had given the agents another valuable lead.

"After the gang had the ransom money," he said, "they put me into their car. I was blindfolded. We drove round and round. I guess they did this so I would never be able to trace their hideaway. They stopped once when the driver said they

KATE BARKER
ALIAS "MA" BARKER

- Leader of Barker-Karpis Gang.
- She guided her 4 sons, Fred, Herman, Lloyd and "Doc" Barker into careers of crime.

needed gas. But they didn't stop at a gasoline station. After they stopped, one of the men took three or four tin cans out of the trunk rack of the car and filled the gas tank from them. Then I think they threw the tin cans away."

"If we could find those cans, we might find fingerprints," Mr. Hoover said, and he asked his agents and the local police for a hundred miles around to look for some empty gasoline cans alongside the road. If those cans could be found, Mr. Hoover knew that they would tell a story to the F.B.I. fingerprint experts.

6 SMASHING THE "MA" BARKER GANG

The next day four large gasoline cans were found at the side of a road about fifty miles from St. Paul. The cans were flown to Washington and hurried into the Identification Division of the F.B.I. One fingerprint was found. Within a few minutes Mr. Hoover received a phone call.

"The print is from the right index finger of Arthur 'Doc' Barker, one of the four sons of 'Ma' Barker," he was told. Now Mr. Hoover knew that he had been right all along. This kidnaping had been engineered by "Ma" Barker and carried out by her sons with the probable assistance of Alvin Karpis.

Meanwhile, G-men had been searching for the four red lights which Walter Magee had seen on the left side of the road. They found four flashlights. Good investigative work by the G-men revealed that the flashlights had been sold by the

Grand Silver store in St. Paul. The salesgirl who had sold them a week before was able to describe the man who had bought them.

"Sounds like a description of Alvin Karpis," an F.B.I. agent said. He showed the girl a dozen pictures of wanted criminals. She looked at them and then pointed excitedly to the picture of Alvin Karpis.

"That's the man who bought the flashlights," she announced.

Now at least the G-men knew for whom they were looking. But where were the members of the gang? They had probably separated. More than likely "Ma" Barker had fled to one of her hideouts. These vicious criminals seemed to know just how to avoid the watchful eyes of the F.B.I., but there was one thing the gang did not know. They did not know that J. Edgar Hoover had a list of the numbers of the ransom bills. Every bank in the Midwest had the same list.

Before long some of the bills turned up in Chicago; others turned up in Toledo and in Cleveland. Gradually the G-men were closing in. They were shadowing every known hoodlum and gangster in the Midwest, hoping that sooner or later one of these would lead the F.B.I. to members of the "Ma" Barker-Alvin Karpis gang.

Then came an important break in the case. Late one night the body of a criminal named Fred Goetz was found on the streets of Cicero, Illinois. Goetz, who had been killed by a shotgun blast, was known to have been a member of the gang. It looked now as if the gang were falling out. Agents were assigned to digging up every possible bit of information about the dead gangster who, ironically enough, was known as "Shotgun" Goetz.

They talked to the people in the rooming house in Cicero where Goetz had lived. One of these persons said the gangster had once boasted that, together with "Doc" Barker and a man named Volney Davis, he had picked up the $200,000 in ransom notes from the side of the road. The F.B.I. distributed pictures of known members of the gang to all parts of the country. In every post office in America these pictures were placed over the sign, "Wanted by the F.B.I."

Further investigation revealed that Goetz had often visited a Dr. Joseph Moran at a hotel in Chicago. Doctor Moran specialized in removing fingerprints and in changing the faces of gangsters. The agents questioned hotel employees about others who had visited Dr. Moran. From the descriptions given, the agents were able to identify Harry Campbell, Oliver Berg, Russell Gibson, James Wilson, and William Harrison—all known to be members of "Ma" Barker's mob. Pictures of these men were sent all over the country, and the Chicago newspapers printed the photographs of all known members of the gang.

This publicity was extremely valuable, for soon the F.B.I. began to receive tips from people who thought they had recognized one or more of the mob. Each tip was followed up closely by the patient G-men. One of them finally brought results. G-men were told that some of the gang were living in an apartment on Pine Grove Avenue in Chicago, and that others were living in an apartment on Surf Street. Both apartments were surrounded by agents of the F.B.I.

The men had no sooner taken their positions than Arthur "Doc" Barker walked out of the house with Mildred Kuhlman, one of the women who associated with the gang. "Doc" Barker didn't have a chance to draw his gun. Both he and the woman were handcuffed and hurried off to the F.B.I. office to be questioned.

In the meantime other agents had closed in on the Pine Grove Avenue apartment. A Special Agent commanded the occupants to surrender. Clare Gibson, wife of Russell Gibson, Ruth Heidt, and Bryan Bolton complied with this command. Russell Gibson chose to fight it out. He fired a Browning automatic at the agent guarding the door. The agent returned the fire and Gibson fell at the foot of the stairway, mortally wounded.

When the agents searched the apartment they found a small arsenal. There were automatic pistols, police revolvers, two Browning automatic rifles, a 20-gauge shotgun, and a large amount of ammunition. In the apartment there was also a map of Florida with a penciled circle around the town of Ocala. The agents also learned that Karpis and Fred Barker were hunting an alligator known as "old Joe."

Within two hours a special squad of agents was en route to Ocala. They learned that there was an alligator known as "old Joe" in the vicinity. Also, they found that a man resembling Fred Barker and a woman resembling his mother were living in a cottage on Lake Weir. When, early one morning, G-men surrounded the hideout, the inspector in charge called to its occupants to surrender. The only answer was a blast of machine-gun fire from the house. The G-men fired back. Again the inspector in charge cried out for those inside to surrender. The answer was the same.

Ten agents now rained fire into the cottage, and then suddenly everything was quiet. They entered the house. Two bodies riddled with bullets lay on the floor—"Ma" Barker and her son Fred had come to the end of the road. Fourteen thousand dollars, part of the ransom money, was found in the house.

7 THE CAPTURE OF "PUBLIC ENEMY NUMBER ONE"

Headlines in newspapers all over the country screamed, "Ma Barker and her son killed by G-men." Alvin Karpis and Harry Campbell, who were hiding in Miami, trembled when they saw the headlines. They were like most criminals who spend the greater part of their time hiding, running, and shaking when they hear a knock on the door. Karpis and Campbell had plenty of money, but what good was it when they were "Wanted by the F.B.I."? They decided to drive to Atlantic City in New Jersey.

They bought a second-hand car and started north. But the G-men soon found out the license number of their automobile and sent word of it to every police chief in the country.

One morning a policeman in Atlantic City caught sight of the car in a garage. He told his chief and the Atlantic City police moved into action. They learned the identities of the two men who had put the car in the garage and traced them to the Hotel Danmor. There it was found that Karpis had registered under the name of Carson, while Campbell had registered as Cameron. The police were excited by this discovery. It looked as though they would soon have their hands on Alvin Karpis, Public Enemy Number 1, and Harry Campbell, desperate kidnaper and murderer. They knocked on the door of the hotel room where the two men were staying, thinking that the criminals would come out quietly.

The door opened, but Karpis and Campbell came out shooting. Then the two criminals dashed down the stairs to the street. They ran to a nearby garage and made off with a Pontiac sedan. Soon they were speeding out of the city. Now the G-men had to start all over again.

The two criminals drove to Quakertown, Pennsylvania, where they abandoned their stolen car and set about to get another. Soon they saw a man getting out of his car, and they went up to him.

Pointing a Tommy gun, Karpis growled, "Get back in the car and drive where I tell you."

"I'm a doctor on a sick call," the man protested.

"Get back in there and drive, or you'll be the one who'll be sick," Karpis said.

The doctor, whose name was Horace H. Hunsicker, was forced into his car and made to drive all the way to Ohio. Then Karpis and Campbell let him go and continued alone to Toledo. There they hid for several weeks before they joined forces with a man with the queer nickname of "Burrhead." His real name was George Keady, but everyone called him "Burrhead" because his hair stuck up like the needles on a porcupine.

Karpis now had dreams of organizing a new gang as big and powerful as the one that "Ma" Barker had headed. But first he needed money, so he, Campbell, and "Burrhead" held up a mail truck at Warren, Ohio, and escaped with $72,000 in loot. Karpis then took on another partner-in-crime named Sam Coker, a crook named Fred Hunter, and a criminal named John Brock who was wanted by the police of a dozen states.

Now that he had a gang of his own, Karpis planned new crimes. They robbed a train in Ohio,

ALVIN KARPIS

- Member of Barker-Karpis Gang.
- Criminal career dated from 1926. Included arrests for burglary, auto theft and kidnaping.
- Participated in Bremer and other kidnapings.
- Apprehended by Director Hoover and F.B.I. Agents on May 1, 1936, in New Orleans, Louisiana.
- Serving life sentence in Federal Penitentiary.

getting $34,000. When the F.B.I. heard the details of this robbery, they had a hunch that it had been done by Alvin Karpis and his new gang.

After the train robbery, Karpis did something new. He hired an airplane to take two members of his gang and himself to Hot Springs, Arkansas. Nevertheless, this trip was to furnish the F.B.I. with a clue, for immediately after a big robbery G-men try to find out how the criminals got away. As a matter of routine they now checked all the airports in that part of Ohio and as a result learned of a pilot who had flown three men to Hot Springs four days after the robbery. When the flier described his passengers, the G-men knew that they were Karpis, Fred Hunter and John Brock.

At once the G-men hurried to Hot Springs. The two robbers had already gone, but it was learned that Karpis had done a lot of talking about deep-sea fishing. In the cottage where he had stayed the G-men found books on fishing and pamphlets describing fishing in Florida and other southern waters.

Karpis and his gang knew that the F.B.I. was after them. They had to keep moving, for if they stayed in one place too long the G-men would catch up with them. They hid out in New Orleans.

By this time Alvin Karpis' mother probably wouldn't have recognized him. "Doc" Moran had done plastic surgery on his face. Karpis' nose, broken in an early gang fight, had been straightened. Now he brushed his hair straight back and wore glasses. As a matter of fact, the fiendish killer who hated the whole world looked like a mild-mannered college professor.

He fooled everyone but the F.B.I. They knew that there was one thing Karpis loved to do. He loved deep-sea fishing, and the books and pamphlets found in his Hot Springs cottage told the F.B.I. where to look for him. At once G-men covered many Florida and Louisiana fishing resorts. Narrowing their search down to New Orleans, they found there a fisherman who had taken two men out to fish in the Gulf several times. The G-men knew what Karpis looked like, in spite of his plastic surgery. Railroad men who had been on the train robbed by Karpis and his gang had given them a good description of the criminal's new appearance.

The fisherman said that one of his two passengers—the man he knew as "Mr. O'Hara"—seemed to answer Karpis' description. G-men went to every shop in New Orleans that sold fishing tackle. They found one shopkeeper who had sold a rod and a reel to a man who gave the name of O'Hara.

Eventually they found that "Mr. O'Hara" owned a car. Some person who was interviewed by the G-men remembered the number of the license plate. While the F.B.I. agents searched the city for a car bearing that license number, J. Edgar Hoover arrived in New Orleans to take active charge of the case. He summoned thirty extra agents to help. And then one day an agent cruising in an F.B.I. car spotted the license number they were all looking for. It was on a car that was parked in front of an apartment house at 3343 Canal Street.

F.B.I. cars look like ordinary automobiles. They are usually Fords or Plymouths or Chevrolets. From the outside they don't look like police cars. But if you were to look under the hood you would find that the engine had been stepped up so that the car could travel one hundred miles an hour. On the dashboard you would find a two-way radio, and on the floor a siren button.

When the agent and his partner spotted the car,

they quickly reported this to the Director of the F.B.I.

"Park a hundred yards away and keep the car in sight," Mr. Hoover said tersely. "We'll be there immediately."

Mr. Hoover and his assistant, Clyde Tolson, were on the way to the apartment within ten minutes with the special squad of agents. As the F.B.I. car hurried to Canal Street, Mr. Hoover gave orders. He knew that Alvin Karpis had sworn never to be taken alive. The gangster would shoot it out as he had shot it out with the police in Atlantic City. Mr. Hoover didn't want any of his men to be shot at— they were too valuable for that. And he wanted Karpis taken alive.

He gave orders that the block on which the apartment house stood was to be surrounded. Then he ordered agents to take their stations at the back of the house. He threw a net around the hideout. Not even a fish could have escaped from this net. When he arrived at the scene, he waited until all of his men had taken their assigned positions.

"We want him alive," Mr. Hoover said. "But shoot if you have to defend yourself."

Mr. Hoover was sure that he and his men were

in for a desperate gun battle. Before the fight was over many of his men might be wounded or killed. He tried not to think of that. He knew every one of these agents well. He had seen many of them grow from inexperienced young students into calm, efficient, sharp-shooting G-men. Yet sometimes he had to give them orders that meant they might be killed. This was such a time. But when risks had to be run, he himself ran them, too. He was well aware of his present danger, for Alvin Karpis had boasted that one day he would "get Hoover." Well, now he was to have his chance.

Mr. Hoover decided to approach the house from a southerly direction with Clyde Tolson, the Associate Director of the F.B.I. Two other agents were to approach from the opposite direction. The four men would meet in front of the house and go up to Apartment 1 on the first floor. If all four were killed, Karpis and his gang would still have to face G-men in the back of the house and the others who were guarding both ends of the street. The Atlantic City police had made the mistake of trying to capture Karpis and Campbell alone. Mr. Hoover never made that mistake. He always thought of raids such as this one as teamwork. Every man had a job. If he did it properly, the team would accomplish what it had set out to do. And when the F.B.I. makes raids, the highest ranking official by tradition always goes in first. When the Director is on the scene, he always heads the raid.

Now the raiders began to close in. As Mr. Hoover and his associate approached in their car, two men came out of the house. At least twenty G-men spotted and recognized this pair as Alvin Karpis and Fred Hunter, but the two men were not aware of it for there was no excitement, no shooting. The G-men were afraid that if guns were fired, innocent bystanders might be killed.

Suddenly the watching G-men grew tense. A man leading an old white horse came slowly along the street. Rather than wait any longer and take chances, Mr. Hoover jumped out of his car and dashed for Karpis and Hunter.

Karpis literally froze in his tracks when he looked up and saw, coming toward him, the man he had boasted he would kill.

"You're both under arrest," the Director said quietly. "Put up your hands."

Karpis' hands shot up. Fred Hunter looked startled. He turned his head quickly, all set to run.

Then he looked again at J. Edgar Hoover.

"Okay, okay," he cried in fear. "I'll surrender."

Not a shot had been fired; not a voice had been raised. Automobiles passing didn't even slow down. Their drivers never knew that two of the most dangerous criminals in history were being led to an F.B.I. car at the curb.

Karpis and Hunter were driven back to the F.B.I. office.

"Well, it took a lot of you to catch me," Karpis snarled. "After all, I was Public Enemy Number One."

"You were nothing but Public Rat Number One," J. Edgar Hoover said with contempt.

With the capture of Alvin Karpis the "Ma" Barker-Alvin Karpis gang was completely broken. In all, twenty-six members of the mob were tried and sent to jail. Six, including Karpis, were given life sentences. The only one the G-men never caught was "Doc" Moran, but members of the gang caught up with him before they were captured. They felt that "Doc" Moran knew too much, so they killed him.

Young agents like J—— S—— who studied the

"Ma" Barker-Alvin Karpis case afterward learned that there is no substitute for thorough, plodding work. The G-men had been put on the trail of the Barker gang when Mr. Bremer remembered that his kidnapers had filled their gasoline tank from tin cans. This was the first break in their case. When the cans were found, the fingerprint of "Doc" Barker on one of them told that the Barker gang was involved in the kidnaping. The second break came when the girl who had sold four flashlights identified a picture of Alvin Karpis as the man who had made the purchase.

The big break came after Karpis and his new gang had robbed the train. When the G-men found out that a private plane had flown Karpis to Hot Springs, it put them on his trail. Knowing that he liked deep-sea fishing, they went south and caught him in New Orleans.

The police of many foreign countries studied the Barker-Karpis case, for it was a perfect example of thorough, intelligent investigative work. It was also a perfect example of teamwork. The special agents in the field were always in close touch with J. Edgar Hoover in Washington. The F.B.I. laboratories were open twenty-four hours a day investigating various clues sent in by the men in the field.

If you were to ask J. Edgar Hoover to name the agent who was chiefly responsible for solving the case, he would laugh.

"We don't work that way," he'd tell you. "In football, the man who makes the long run to make a touchdown is the one who gets the headlines. But he couldn't have made that run if it hadn't been for the other ten men on his team. It was like that when we caught the Barker-Karpis gang. Fifty men here in the laboratory and the Identification Division played their parts. Every agent in the country was on the alert during our hunt for these rats. A hundred of them contributed scraps of information. Here in Washington we put all the little scraps together and gradually they formed a picture of the whole gang.

"Incidentally, don't forget that the local police in Chicago and Toledo and Miami and a dozen other cities worked with us. They deserve part of the credit, too."

Mr. Hoover's expression changed to one of great seriousness. "When a gang like the Barker-Karpis mob starts a campaign of robbery, murder, kidnaping," he said, "they are really declaring war against our country. We have to fight such a gang just as our army would fight an enemy in battle. And when we're fighting a gang, we know that every law-abiding man and woman in the country is on our side. During the hunt for the Barker-Karpis mob we received hundreds of tips from private citizens. We never revealed their names. But believe me, we could never fight and destroy such gangs if we didn't have the help of every police force in the country and of the people of the United States."

Alvin Karpis, spending the rest of his life in prison, must wonder now and then how different his life would have been if he had accepted the invitation of the Y.M.C.A. secretary. Mr. Hoover was curious about how the other members of the original teen-age gang had turned out. He investigated and discovered that all of the boys who had joined the Y.M.C.A. are respected citizens of Topeka. They are lawyers, doctors, businessmen—not one has ever been accused of any crime. The

Y.M.C.A. had benefited them. Mr. Hoover later told Karpis how well his teen-age pals had done.

"I guess," Karpis said bitterly, "they were the smart ones. I was the dope."

8 THE F.B.I. NATIONAL ACADEMY

Police departments all over the country were impressed by the brilliant work done by the F.B.I. in destroying the horrible gangs of the early 1930's and solving so many kidnapings and bank robberies. Many police chiefs wrote to Mr. Hoover asking if they could go to Washington to study some of the new methods used by the F.B.I. Only a few months before the capture of Alvin Karpis, the F.B.I. National Academy had been founded.

Police from all over the country now began to attend the Academy to learn the F.B.I. methods in a course similar to the one taken by J— S— and the other young agents. Up to the present time more than 4,000 police officers have been graduated from the National Academy.

At the Academy, the F.B.I. holds two courses a year of twelve weeks each for policemen from all over the country. Usually about eighty men en-

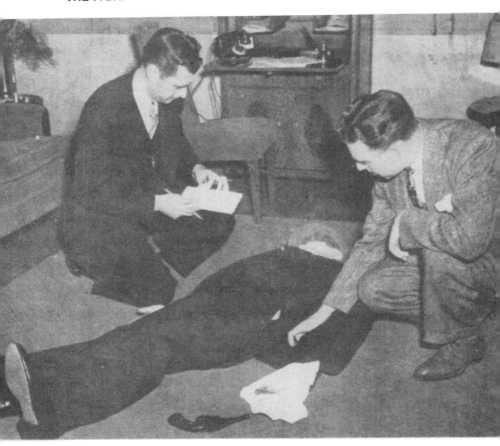

Crime Scene Room showing examination at the scene of a hypothetical crime, Training School, Federal Bureau of Investigation, United States Department of Justice.

roll for each training period. Most of the classes are taught by actual F.B.I. agents, each a specialist in his own field. But some outside lecturers in specialized fields are also used.

The F.B.I. instructors insist upon one thing. Each student is asked to write down in a thick notebook everything that he learns in his classes. Every few days the instructors examine these notebooks carefully so that when a man graduates, his book is filled with accurate notes and information. When he returns home to teach his fellow policemen what he has learned, the notebook serves as a textbook.

Most of the officers who attend the F.B.I. National Academy are already experienced policemen when they arrive to take the course. Although they are fully acquainted with the routine of police work, they know little about the use of new scientific methods of detection. This is one of the subjects they learn at the Academy. They also learn a great deal about shooting that they never knew before.

"Never fire your gun while you are running," the firearms instructor tells them over and over again. "If you do, your aim will be bad and you may hit some innocent person."

A portion of the firearms reference collection in the F.B.I. Laboratory.

This bit of advice has saved the lives of many National Academy graduates. When a policeman is running after a criminal, the advantage is on the side of the lawbreaker, who may suddenly stop, turn, take careful aim, and fire.

To get the better of the man he is pursuing, the policeman is taught to get as close to the running criminal as possible and then to stop, sink to one knee, aim, and fire. Some men can aim best in a kneeling position. Others aim better standing up. At the Academy the police are taught to turn their bodies sidewise when they fire, thus giving the criminal a narrower target.

These are little hints that help to make the job of a policeman easier and safer. When the old-time policeman cornered a criminal in a hotel room or a cottage, he started shooting away. He was brave and he wanted to shoot it out with the man he had cornered. The F.B.I. has taught the police that this is an unwise way to catch a murderer. To begin with, a criminal should, if possible, be caught alive, for there is always the chance that he will name his accomplices and thus help the police solve perhaps a dozen robberies. Dead men never talk, and a dead criminal is no good as a witness.

At the Academy law enforcement officers learn how to plan a raid. If the police in Atlantic City had had more time to plan the raid on the hotel where Alvin Karpis and Harry Campbell were hiding, they would have had a better opportunity of apprehending them.

The men attending the National Academy spend long hours in the Fingerprint Identification Building. There they learn, among other things, to cope with the criminals who in recent years have become expert in disguising themselves. Because of his skill at disguise, Willie Sutton, the bank robber who is now serving thirty years in jail, was called "Willie the Actor."

Sutton studied the art of make-up the way an actor studies it. He never used a mask. He just changed the look of his face every time he robbed a bank. He could flatten his nose by forcing putty into his nostrils. He could make his face fatter by sticking wads of cotton between his upper teeth and the skin of his cheeks. He could dye his hair. But there are certain things that no criminal can disguise.

He can't change the shape of his head. He can't change his height or his size. He can't very well

Simulation of raiding operation, using magnetic blackboard, in training Special Agents, Federal Bureau of Investigation, United States Department of Justice.

change the shape of his ears, and it is almost impossible for him to change either his handwriting or his voice. The police attending school at the Academy learn the tricks criminals use to change their looks.

When the eighty men in each class are graduated and return home, each one teaches perhaps another eighty fellow officers how the F.B.I. operates. Because of this, only the brightest policemen are selected to attend the Academy. The local heads of law enforcement agencies also consider an officer's past schooling when choosing men for the Academy because Mr. Hoover has stated that he has found that high-school and college graduates make the best teachers.

Some of the men who have attended the Academy are sent back again and again for special courses. Mr. Hoover has often said that brains, science, and hard work are more powerful weapons to use against a criminal than Tommy guns or tear gas.

There was a time when a robbery, a murder, or even a kidnaping was thought to be a "local crime." Years ago old-time police chiefs wanted no outside help. They didn't even want the state police to

An examiner in the F.B.I. Laboratory comparing the heel of a suspect's ▶
shoe with that of a cast made at the scene of a crime.

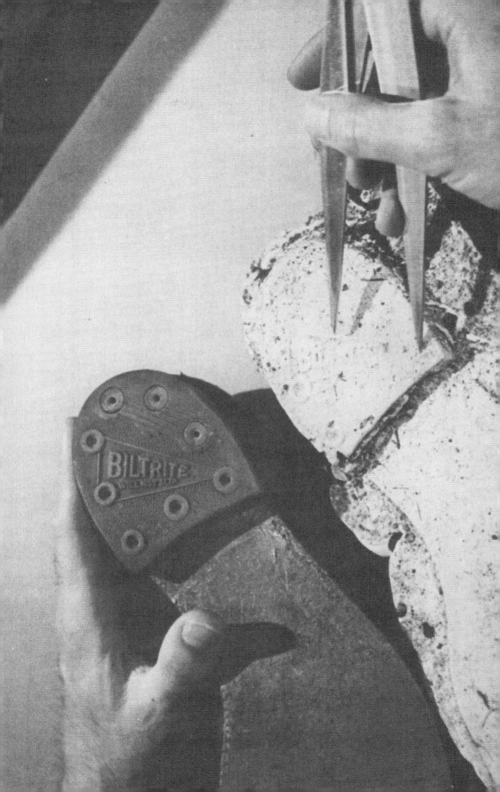

interfere. But gradually they have learned that there is really no such thing as a "local crime." A gang might plan to rob a bank in your home town. Its members might plan the crime in Los Angeles, a thousand miles from the bank they intend to rob. They fly to your home town and hide a getaway car somewhere. After robbing the bank, they hop into the car and speed across the state line to hide in some large city.

The local police are helpless in such a case, so they have learned to call in the F.B.I. Perhaps one of the robbers may be identified as having come from Los Angeles. If so, the F.B.I. agents in that city will investigate. As often as not they will find the names and descriptions of the members of the gang. Next they will broadcast a description of each man all over the country. They will get the serial number of the bills stolen, and every bank in the United States will start watching for persons who may try to pass such bills. The local police force does not have the manpower, the money, or the time to do all this.

It is impossible to transport the huge F.B.I. laboratory in Washington to every community in the country, but the F.B.I. does the next best thing. It teaches the Academy-trained men how to use that laboratory. An Academy-trained man on a local police force knows exactly what type of information to give the F.B.I. concerning robberies and wanted criminals. He also knows how the F.B.I. can help him and his local police force to solve crimes.

One police officer from a small town in North Carolina graduated from the Academy and returned home to find that a brutal murder had been committed the day before. His police chief told him to take charge of it. A suspect was being held, but he had what seemed a perfect alibi, and he stoutly protested his innocence. The police had the murder gun, but there were no fingerprints on it.

"There is nothing to connect this suspect with the murder," the chief said, "but he was known to hate the dead man and to have threatened him. But we can't prove a thing against him."

The Academy graduate studied the gun carefully. He looked at it through a microscope. He noticed that one small piece of thread was stuck to the trigger. He never would have bothered with

Tire and heel print examination, F.B.I. Headquarters, Washington, D.C.

a small piece of thread before he had taken the Academy course. But now he forwarded it to the F.B.I. laboratory together with the suspect's coat. He also told the F.B.I. that the suspect was left-handed.

Within twenty-four hours he received a tele-typed report from the F.B.I. laboratory stating that there were minute traces of oil in the left-hand pocket of the coat. The oil on the gun matched the oil in the pocket. The small piece of thread? It had come loose from the coat pocket and had stuck to the gun. It was obvious that this suspect had carried the gun in the left-hand pocket of the coat.

Confronted with this evidence, the prisoner confessed. The police chief wrote a letter to J. Edgar Hoover telling him that the murder never would have been solved if his subordinate hadn't studied modern laboratory methods in the Academy course.

Today Academy-trained officers are scattered all over the country. This makes the job of the F.B.I. much easier. If they move into a city in pursuit of a gang, they immediately get in touch with the local police. If the police chief is an Academy graduate, he will know just how the F.B.I. operates. If the Special Agent in Charge says, "Chief, we have located five dangerous men holed up in a house just outside of town and need your help," the chief doesn't send a few men to storm the house. He does it the F.B.I. way, and the chances are that no matter how desperate the criminals are or how many guns they have, no officer will be hurt.

Once a reporter said to J. Edgar Hoover, "You worry more about the safety of your men than I do about my own kids."

The Director of the F.B.I. grinned. But he was serious almost immediately. "You know," he said, "it costs the taxpayers thousands of dollars to train an F.B.I. man. I can't allow any of them to be killed because they are too valuable to the country. Besides, the lives of my men are very precious to their families. I have no right to risk those lives unless I'm forced to."

9 THE CASE OF THE GERMAN SPY RING

The F.B.I. went to war long before Pearl Harbor thrust the whole country into World War II. Spies do their best work in peacetime, and J. Edgar Hoover knew that there were plenty of German spies in this country in the 1930's. President Roosevelt knew it, too, and feared that they would place us in grave danger if we were ever attacked by an enemy. It was to the F.B.I. that he gave the task of protecting our country against foreign spies and saboteurs.

There was immediate work to do, for German agents had organized a pro-Nazi group called the German-American Bund which had chapters in every large American city. The F.B.I. kept a sharp watch on this organization, and some good citizens joined it and then kept the F.B.I. informed as to what was going on. They became accepted as real

Nazis, and gradually they learned all the secrets of the Bund.

The Bund members always carried American flags in their parades, just as the Communists do today. This practice was good camouflage. The Bund was no more American than the Communist Party is today, but it fooled a lot of well-meaning German-Americans who thought that the organization was trying to promote friendship between this country and Germany.

The G-men, who had closely watched the Bund, which had loyal Americans in it, soon had the names of everyone in the United States who belonged to the organization. This was to come in mighty handy one day.

The F.B.I. was greatly aided in its work by the many Americans of German birth or parentage who were loyal citizens of the United States. One of these was a man named Harry Sawyer. Born in Germany, he left there in 1921 and in 1936 became a naturalized American citizen. In 1939 Sawyer decided to visit his mother in Germany. Upon landing in Hamburg, he was arrested by the German Gestapo, the greatly feared secret police that operated under the Hitler dictatorship. Then Sawyer was taken to the Gestapo headquarters.

"I'm an American citizen," he said angrily. "You have no right to arrest me."

"Once a German, always a German," the Gestapo officer in charge sneered. "We know all about you. You have been working in an airplane factory in America. Is that right?"

"That's right," Sawyer replied, puzzled.

"You can be useful to us," the officer said. "You can go now, but you will hear from us later."

Harry Sawyer went on to visit his mother. He found that she was quite sick, so he decided to stay in Germany until she had recovered. Three months later he was contacted by the Gestapo again and told that he would have to return to America to act as a spy for Germany.

"Sooner or later we will be at war with the United States," the Gestapo agents told Sawyer. "We have a large spy organization in America now. You will join it. If you do not, something very serious will happen to your mother."

Sawyer thought for a while and then agreed to do anything the Gestapo wished. First he was sent to a training school in Hamburg run by a master spy, Major Nickolaus Ritter. Sawyer studied everything there was to learn about sabotage, invisible writing, and almost invisible cameras. He learned how to operate a short-wave radio so he could send messages back to Germany. When he had finished his training, his German bosses gave him a list of agents with whom he would work in the United States. Sawyer was then given instructions to return to New York.

"All right," he agreed. "I will try to do a good job for you. Heil Hitler!"

"Heil Hitler!" Major Ritter said. "You will leave for New York on Thursday."

"I'd better stop in at the American Consulate to see that my passport is in order," Sawyer suggested. "We don't want any slip-up on that."

"You're right," Ritter said approvingly. "Never let the Americans suspect that you are working for your fatherland."

Harry Sawyer went to the American Consulate that afternoon. But he didn't go to the Passport Division. He knew very well that his passport was in order; it always had been.

Instead, he asked to see the American Consul. The United States government sends an American ambassador, minister, or other representative, to the capital of every foreign country. But in all large cities of the world it maintains offices called consulates. The person in charge of one of our consulates is an American consul, and it is his duty to look after the interests of any American citizens who happen to be in that foreign city. That is why Sawyer, who said he was an American citizen in trouble, was led directly to the American Consul.

"I wanted to see you, sir," Harry Sawyer said earnestly, "because I am a German spy on my way to the United States. When I reach there, I am to get information concerning ship movements, military establishments, war production, new airplanes, and the progress of something I don't understand very well. My German superiors say that this strange thing, which is called heavy water, is being experimented with at Columbia University in New York. I'm supposed to establish a short-wave radio station on Long Island and send all my messages to Germany from there."

"You're a German agent?" The Consul exploded. "Why have you come to me?"

"The Nazis think that I'm a German agent,"

Sawyer said softly, "but although I was born in Germany I'm an American citizen. I love the United States, and I'll do anything I can to help fight the Nazis. That's why I've come to you."

"You are a good American, Mr. Sawyer," the Consul said gravely. "This is a matter for the F.B.I. I will inform them when you are to arrive in New York. You will be met by F.B.I. agents."

"That's a great load off my mind," Sawyer said, relieved.

He took the next ship for New York. Upon landing, he was met by two agents of the F.B.I. They went to a hotel and registered. Little was said until they reached the privacy of the hotel room.

Then one of the agents, whom we shall call F—— P——, smiled and said, "My name is F—— P——. Our American Consul in Hamburg told us all about you, Mr. Sawyer. If you'll do as we say, you can make a great contribution to your country."

"That's all I want to do," Sawyer said simply.

"Sit down and tell us all about it," the agent suggested.

Sawyer told the story from the beginning. He gave the two F.B.I. agents the names of the few

German agents of whom he had knowledge. Then he handed them his wrist watch. He pried off the back of it.

"Here are a dozen tiny microfilms," said Sawyer. "I am to deliver these to three people. They are Colonel Duquesne and Lilly Stein of New York City, and Everett Roeder of Merrick, Long Island. I am also to get in touch with Herman Lang in Glendale, Long Island. He's employed by the L. C. Norden Company and does highly secret work in connection with the Norden bombsight."

"What 'cover' have the Germans ordered you to take?" F—— P—— asked. In F.B.I. language, a "cover" is a disguise for a person's true activities.

"They told me to rent an office in New York," Sawyer said, "and pose as a consulting engineer. I am to stay in that office eight hours a day, and various German agents are to contact me there."

"Office space is hard to get in New York," F—— P—— told Sawyer, "but I think we can find a place for you. Meanwhile, we will photograph all of your microfilms. They appear to be covered with writing in code."

"I forgot to tell you," Sawyer said, "that I know the code, too. Here's a copy of it."

Within an hour the microfilms had been photographed and decoded and were hidden once more in Sawyer's watch. The next day the G-men found an office for Sawyer on West Forty-second Street and rented one for themselves next door. They had wired Sawyer's office for sound and had put an X-ray mirror in the wall between the two offices. It permitted an F.B.I. agent to see through the wall and even take photographs of anyone who came into Sawyer's office, although the G-man himself could not be seen.

Now the trap was baited. The F.B.I. waited to see who would walk into it.

Back in Washington J. Edgar Hoover held a meeting of his assistant directors. They all knew that there were German agents working in this country, and they had the names of hundreds of suspects who were members of the German-American Bund. The F.B.I., however, had no proof that any of these persons had actually performed the work of a spy.

"This looks really big," Mr. Hoover said to his men. "Harry Sawyer should lead us to every Ger-

Two-way mirror used by the F.B.I. in the Duquesne case.

man espionage agent in America. But we must work slowly and carefully if we are to get hold of the big fish."

He gave crisp orders. Anyone who visited Sawyer's office was to be followed. Dozens of F.B.I. agents who were experts at "shadowing" people were now assigned to New York City. This watchfulness was rewarded when Colonel Duquesne finally visited Sawyer at his office. The Nazi agent proved to be crafty, sly, and very boastful.

"Just to show you what we have been doing, Sawyer," he said while F.B.I. agents in the next room listened, "here are the plans of a new type of bomb being produced in the United States. I photographed the documents in a plant in Delaware."

"You are certainly smart, Colonel!" Sawyer exclaimed. Then, following the G-men's orders, he handed the microfilms to Duquesne. Quite pleased with his success, Duquesne left the office, completely unaware that two men were following him.

In time, other spies came to Sawyer's office for instructions; among them were Lilly Stein, Everett Roeder, and Herman Lang. All were photographed by the magic eye of the camera that could take pictures through walls, while a tape recorder took down everything the visitors said. When they left, each one was followed. Soon the F.B.I. knew who the spies' friends were.

Every week the F.B.I. would give Sawyer information about airplane production, ship movements, and new military weapons. This information was sent to Germany by means of the Long Island short-wave radio. Of course every bit of the information was carefully prepared and harmless, but back in Hamburg, Major Nickolaus Ritter was well pleased with the work of his agent, Harry Sawyer.

Now Sawyer told Colonel Duquesne that he wanted the name of every German agent in the country.

Duquesne smiled. "I am the only one who has all that information," he boasted. Then he went on:

"Paul Fehse is in charge of the marine division of our espionage system. He is coming in to see you tomorrow. At present he is working on an American ship as a cook, but when we go to war against these American swine, he will be in charge

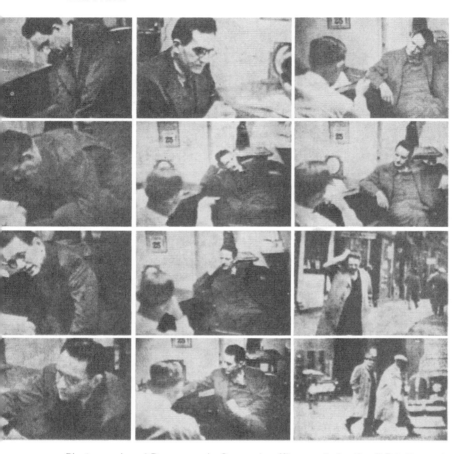

Photographs of Duquesne in Sawyer's office made by the F.B.I. through the two-way mirror.

of sabotaging American shipping. There are thirty-one other agents working here. But I won't give you their names."

"Have we only thirty-two agents in the United States?" Sawyer asked.

"That's all we have at the moment," and Duquesne laughed. "But every one of us is an expert, a trained agent. Helping us are hundreds of German-Americans and others who don't know that we are spies. These poor fools are either pacifists or Americans of German birth who think they are promoting friendship between our countries."

During the weeks that followed, Sawyer learned the names of a few of the other agents. The F.B.I. checked up on every one of these, and gradually, by hard work, managed to obtain a pretty complete picture of the entire set-up.

The time was June, 1941. Although the United States was not yet at war, President Roosevelt, General Marshall, and J. Edgar Hoover knew that sooner or later either Japan or Germany would attack us. It was time to pull in the net and catch the fish. Mr. Hoover decided to spring the trap on Saturday, June 28, 1941.

On that day more than two hundred G-men

LEFT: Photograph of Frederick Duquesne taken July 1, 1940, by F.B.I. agents.
RIGHT: Photograph of Frederick Duquesne in earlier days found in his possession when he was arrested June 28, 1941.

LEFT: Frederick Duquesne and Harry Sawyer, taken by F.B.I. agents May 29, 1940.
RIGHT: Frederick Duquesne, taken May 29, 1940, by F.B.I. agents.

swooped down on the German agents. Some were in New York, others on Long Island, and still others in Philadelphia, Chicago, Los Angeles, and Boston. Every single one of the thirty-three was caught. Nineteen pleaded guilty—the other fourteen entered pleas of not guilty.

When their trials began, the F.B.I. produced moving pictures of many of them, together with recordings of their voices. All were found guilty. They were sentenced to prison terms totaling more than three hundred years. So ended the career of the biggest spy ring that had ever operated in the United States.

The arrest of the thirty-three spies did not, of course, end the danger. The Germans kept sending more agents to this country. Many pretended that they were refugees—unfortunate people who were forced to leave Germany because they were anti-Nazi. But usually the F.B.I. had advance information and was on hand when these persons landed. Within the next few months nine important agents and dozens of small fry were arrested.

10 OUTWITTING SOME SABOTEURS

Then came the shots that were heard all around the world. The Japanese attacked Pearl Harbor December 7, 1941, and we were finally in a shooting war. J. Edgar Hoover was given one of the most difficult and important jobs in the country. He and his men were to assist in devising methods to protect the plants and factories that were producing our airplanes, guns, ships, and bombs. He was also responsible for the apprehension of alien enemies in the United States, Puerto Rico, and the Virgin Islands. The nationals of Japan, Germany, Italy, Bulgaria, Hungary, and Rumania were proclaimed alien enemies.

By nightfall on the day following the bombing of Pearl Harbor, 1,771 of the country's most dangerous enemy aliens had been taken into custody. During the entire wartime period, a total of 16,062 enemy aliens were apprehended. The cases of enemy aliens were heard on an individual basis by Enemy Alien Hearing Boards. Based upon the findings of the Alien Hearing Boards, more than 3,200 of the enemy aliens were interned.

Among the contraband seized were 306,247 rounds of ammunition, 4,626 firearms and 5,068 sticks of dynamite and dynamite caps. Other contraband seized included 3,127 short-wave radio sets, 4,245 cameras, 1,200 swords and daggers, 10 sets of brass knuckles, and a number of maps, charts, code books and military uniforms.

Meanwhile, America had become the arsenal of democracy. Planes, battleships, tanks, and the weapons needed by our allies were being made in American factories. The destruction of these war plants would be a great aid to Germany, and Mr. Hoover feared that the Germans would try to land sabotage experts on our shores. To prevent this, the F.B.I. was warned to be constantly on the alert for saboteurs. Local police forces, state troopers, and the Coast Guard were all alerted and invited to report anything suspicious to the nearest F.B.I. office.

On the night of June 13, 1942, a Coast Guardsman who was patrolling the beach near Amagansett, Long Island, ran into four men. One of them called out a greeting in perfect English. Then the Coast Guardsman heard two of them talking in a foreign language which he didn't understand, but which he thought to be German.

He went back to his headquarters and told his superior officer about these four men.

The Coast Guard officer sent four of his men back to search the beach in the vicinity where the four strangers had been seen. It wasn't long before the Coast Guardsmen saw marks on the sand indicating that something had been buried there. With the aid of shovels they dug up several boxes of explosives, time bombs, dynamite, guns, and other material that could be used in blowing up railroads, bridges, and factories.

That was enough for the Coast Guard officer. This was an F.B.I. matter. He ran for a phone. Within a short time J—— S—— and several other agents were at the scene of the discovery. It seemed clear to them that a submarine had landed the four suspicious characters. It was also plain that they were saboteurs.

But where were the four German agents? J—— S—— hurried to the nearby railroad station at Amagansett. He discovered that four men had taken the train to New York only an hour before. That meant they were now swallowed up in the largest city in the world, mingling with eight million other people!

The F.B.I. feared that the chase might be hopeless, for they knew that German agents were taught not only to speak English well but also to use American slang. J—— S—— admitted he was worried when he reported the story to Washington. Where in New York would he look for these four men? J. Edgar Hoover had the answer.

"They have probably separated and are hiding while awaiting orders to start sabotage," he said.

It was reasoned that the German agents would be unlikely to hide out in Yorkville, which is the German section of New York City. Most of the German-Americans living in Yorkville are as loyal to the United States as people living anywhere else in the country. But it was here that the German-American Bund had its headquarters. And it was here that at least fifteen of the thirty-three spies captured with the help of Harry Sawyer had lived. The saboteurs would look for a safer place.

As it happened, the day after the saboteurs

landed, the New York office of the F.B.I. received a mysterious phone call from a man who said that his name was "Franz Daniel Pastorious." All he would say was that "In about a week I will have important information for you. I will phone your Washington headquarters."

Meanwhile, the F.B.I. agents had smoothed the sand over the beach where the explosives had been dug up. They dug foxholes near by and waited, hoping that the four men who had buried the weapons of sabotage would came back to reclaim them.

On Friday morning, June 19, 1942, the F.B.I. in Washington received a phone call from the mysterious "Franz Daniel Pastorious." By prearrangement the call was quickly switched to the office of J. Edgar Hoover. One of Mr. Hoover's agents talked to the man.

"My real name is George John Dasch," the caller told the agent. "I was landed on the beach at Long Island on June thirteenth with three other men. I have important information for you. Will you send someone to my hotel to whom I can give this information?"

J—— S—— was one of the agents who hurried to

the hotel where George Dasch had registered. Dasch appeared to be a bit frightened. In any case, he had decided to make a full confession. He said that he had been the leader of the four-man sabotage gang. They had come all the way to this country by submarine, and had been put ashore on the beach near Amagansett, Long Island.

"Who were the other three men?" J—— S—— asked.

"Ernest Burger, Heinrich Heinck, and Richard Quirin," Dasch said. "We were all trained in a special sabotage school outside Berlin. Our chief instructor was Lieutenant Walter Kappe. Using incendiary bombs, we learned how to start fires in factories and war plants, and how to blow up bridges. We were taught how to use secret writing and how to use codes. We had to memorize the location of the important war plants and military installations in the United States."

"What were you ordered to do here?" J—— S—— asked.

"We were ordered to blow up plants in Philadelphia, in Tennessee, in New York, and in Illinois. We also had plans to blow up at least a dozen railroad bridges."

"Did your superiors tell you to contact any German spies already in this country?" J—— S—— asked.

Dasch nodded and pulled an ordinary handkerchief from his breast pocket, then handed it to the agent. It looked like an ordinary handkerchief, but the agent's trained eye detected tiny tell-tale marks on it.

"There is secret writing on this handkerchief," he said.

"That's right," Dasch agreed. "You will find there the names of all of our American contacts."

"First of all, tell us where we can find the three men who came here with you," J—— S—— said.

Dasch took a deep breath. "I'll tell you everything," he said. "I know it's the only way I can escape the death penalty."

"I'm not making any promises," J—— S—— said sharply. "We agents are not allowed to do that. But if you tell us the truth, I will see that your co-operation is brought to the attention of the proper authorities."

And then George Dasch sat down and made a complete confession.

"I will tell you where Ernest Burger is hiding," Dasch said, mentioning a New York hotel. "But Burger knows that I was going to contact you. He felt, as I did, that eventually we would be caught, so he and I decided to confess."

"How about the other two—Heinck and Quirin?"

"They will contact Burger and meet him to-morrow," Dasch said.

J—— S—— reached for the phone. He told head-quarters everything he had learned from Dasch.

"We'll start following Burger immediately," headquarters said. "He will lead us to the other two. You stay with Dasch and get everything you can out of him."

J—— S—— went back to questioning Dasch, who by this time couldn't talk fast enough. He described in detail the course of training he had been given in Germany, and J—— S——'s partner took down every word. Dasch was wearing an American-made suit. In his pocket he had a fake draft card that would have fooled anyone. In a money belt he had $82,500 in fifty-dollar bills. He told the agents that when he and his confederates had landed at Long Island, all four had been wearing German marine uniforms.

"If we had been caught then," Dasch said, "you would have had to treat us as prisoners of war because we were in uniform. But as soon as we landed, we buried our uniforms and changed to other clothes we had with us. That's what the Florida group was ordered to do also."

"The Florida group?" J—— S—— was startled. It was the first he'd heard of them!

"They were due to land on June 17th near Jacksonville, in Florida," the German spy said.

"And this is June 19th," J—— S—— said. "Let's go straight to headquarters. I want the Director to hear this."

An hour later George Dasch was telling all he knew about another group of saboteurs. They had been under the command of Edward Kerling. They had left for the United States at about the same time as Dasch and his group.

The F.B.I. had a file on Kerling. Born in Germany, he had been a member of the Bund before the war, and then he had managed to get back to Germany. However, he had lived in this country long enough to speak good English, and for that reason he would be hard to find. The other three members of Kerling's group were Werner Thiel, Hermann Neubauer, and Herbert Haupt. But they might now be going under different names, and Dasch didn't know what those names might be.

Catching them seemed a hopeless job. They might be anywhere in America. But the F.B.I. knew that Herbert Haupt had once lived in Chicago and that he had been a member of the Chicago Bund. The F.B.I. files showed that Herbert Haupt had been investigated by his draft board about a year before, when apparently he had disappeared from Chicago. A routine search had been held then. After all, he might have been an entirely innocent man who had just moved from Chicago without bothering to notify his draft board of his new address. The F.B.I. always gives any suspect the benefit of the doubt. A man is innocent until proven guilty—that's the law of the land and it is always followed closely by the F.B.I.

But now the F.B.I. knew that Haupt's disappearance from Chicago had been no accident. He had slipped back to Germany to join the sabotage group headed by Lieutenant Walter Kappe. Agents were immediately instructed to watch the homes of Haupt's relatives and friends in Chicago in the belief that sooner or later he would show up there.

Meanwhile, the handkerchief which Dasch had given J—— S—— had been treated in the F.B.I. laboratory, revealing the names and addresses of German contacts. G-men were detailed to watch and follow them. This all took place within a few hours—every resource of the F.B.I. was thrown into the job of tracking down the saboteurs. All leaves were canceled. J. Edgar Hoover, Clyde Tolson, and their chief aides never left Washington headquarters. Reports were constantly coming in from Chicago and New York.

On June 20th, the day after Dasch had made his confession, Ernest Burger left his New York hotel and went to a men's furnishing store on Fifth Avenue and Forty-first Street, just across the street from New York's famous Public Library. He was followed by three agents.

Burger went into the store and proceeded to look over some ties. Within a few moments he was joined by two men who answered the description given by Dasch of Heinrich Heinck and Richard Quirin. The three talked for a while, completely unaware that F.B.I. agents were watching them.

Burger left the store first and went back to his hotel. As he started to enter it, an agent went up to him and said, "It's all over, Burger. Come along with me."

Burger looked relieved. Like Dasch, he too was scared. He'd lived in this country long enough to have acquired a healthy respect for the F.B.I.

"I knew you'd get us sooner or later," he said, and he was led to the New York office of the F.B.I.

The remaining two agents followed Heinck and Quirin, hoping that they might lead them to others of the Florida gang. But this did not happen. Heinck and Quirin just went uptown and stood on a street corner for a while. The two agents decided to close in. Heinck and Quirin were dumfounded. They thought they had fooled everyone. The two G-men brought them downtown to the F.B.I. Both Heinck and Quirin were confirmed Nazis. They wouldn't talk.

They didn't have to talk. There was plenty of evidence against them without their saying a word.

It was June 20th. Four German spies had landed in this country on June 13th—now all were behind bars. No one in the country knew what had happened. The strictest secrecy had been kept.

But what of the four men who had landed in Jacksonville, Florida? That's what worried J. Edgar Hoover and his men. For two days nothing happened. Then something really amazing did happen.

A man walked into the Chicago office of the F.B.I. and said that his name was Herbert Haupt. He had just returned from Mexico, where he had spent several months, he said. While there he had received a letter from a friend saying that F.B.I. men had been asking for him to discuss his draft status.

"I've come home now and I've gone to my draft board and cleared up the misunderstanding," Haupt said. "But I just wanted to see if there was anything else you men wanted to know. I've been an American citizen since 1930. I'm a good American," he said with a perfectly straight face, "and if there is anything I can do to help the F.B.I., just let me know."

"As long as you've straightened things out with your draft board," the Special Agent said smoothly, "we have no further interest. I guess it was just one of those little misunderstandings," and the agent smiled.

Herbert Haupt, thinking that his bold move had completely fooled the F.B.I., strode out of the office, unaware that two agents were following him. The next day he bought a second-hand car and had an American flag painted on the windshield. He was never out of sight of F.B.I. men, who hoped he would lead them to other members of the spy ring.

The F.B.I. had been following the persons whose names had been written on Dasch's handkerchief in secret ink. One of them met a man near the Pennsylvania Railroad Station in New York City, and when the agent following him saw the man, he recognized him as Edward Kerling, the leader of the Florida saboteurs. The agent arrested both Kerling and the contact. That was on June 23rd. That same day another contact led F.B.I. agents to Werner Thiel, who was arrested near Grand Central Station.

When Edward Kerling realized that the F.B.I. had enough evidence against him to indict him, he talked freely. He admitted that he and his three companions had landed from a submarine on June 17th at a beach just south of Jacksonville, Florida. They had worn bathing suits and military caps. The latter, they knew, would keep them from being shot as spies, for even a simple army cap constituted a uniform. Kerling stated that his group had buried their explosives and bombs on the beach, just as the Long Island landing party had done, and then he and Werner Thiel had immediately gone to New York. Haupt and the fourth man, Hermann Neubauer, had gone to Chicago.

Less than two hours after the F.B.I. had obtained this information from Kerling, Florida agents had dug up the cache of sabotage weapons.

Meanwhile, agents hurried to the hotel room which had been occupied by Kerling and Thiel. They found $54,550 in cash in the room. Strangely enough, none of the money was counterfeit.

Kerling kept on talking. The F.B.I. agents knew just where they could put their finger on Haupt at any moment, but what about the last man—Hermann Neubauer? He was staying in a Chicago hotel, Kerling said, under the alias of "H. Nicholas."

Within an hour "H. Nicholas" had been found

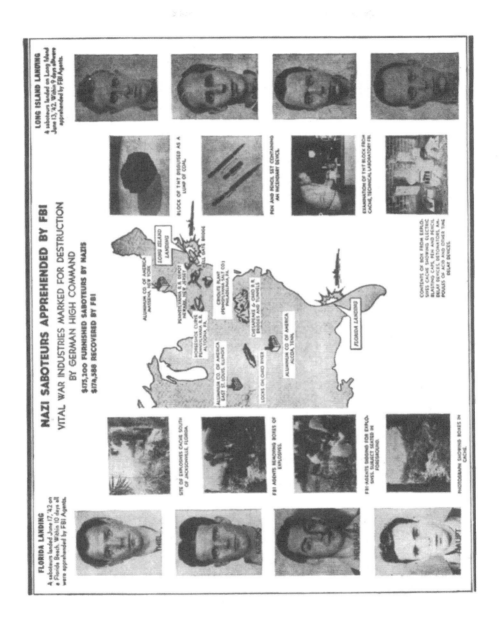

by agents from the Chicago field office of the F.B.I. He surrendered meekly.

And then Herbert Haupt was brought into custody.

Fourteen days after the saboteurs had landed in this country, all eight of them were in jail. It was probably the most brilliant piece of wartime counter-espionage ever on record.

None of the spies had done a single bit of damage. And yet the country went about its daily chores not knowing how close a call the war effort had had. Strict secrecy was maintained until the last of the eight was safely behind bars.

President Roosevelt issued an executive order declaring that the saboteurs should be tried by a military tribunal. These saboteurs were brought to Washington and tried by a court consisting of seven high-ranking Army officers. The prosecutor was Attorney General Francis Biddle. All of the evidence gathered by the G-men was given to Mr. Biddle, who presented it to the seven-man court.

In an effort to save their lives, Dasch and Ernest Burger told everything they knew. They named many targets in the United States which the German High Command considered important enough to blow up. They told the F.B.I. how they were to communicate with their superiors in Germany, and what code they were to use.

All eight men were tried before a military court. All were found guilty and sentenced to death. However, J. Edgar Hoover told President Roosevelt that the information given to the F.B.I. by George Dasch and Ernest Burger was of great importance. He recommended that the President commute their death sentences, and the President did so. The other six were electrocuted.

Thus the F.B.I. faced and met its greatest wartime challenge. The failure of the German agents to land without discovery and to start nationwide sabotage operations was a severe blow to German war plans. The Germans had intended to land saboteurs and hundreds of tons of explosives on American beaches every six weeks. If their plans had succeeded, the United States would have been terrorized by unexplained explosions in plants, railroad stations, bridges, and department stores. The German agents hoped to frighten the American people into forcing leaders to withdraw from the war. For the first time now the German High Command realized that they were being fought by

the F.B.I. All plans for landing additional saboteurs into this country were immediately abandoned.

But if the Nazis gave up any hopes of sabotage,
they did not stop espionage or spying. It was important to the Germans to know about the new
types of bombers and fighter planes we were making. It was important for them to know what progress was being made toward the development of
an atom bomb.

G-men were everywhere during those war
years. We had more than three thousand important factories making the weapons and tanks and
planes and ships that were so badly needed. German agents were trying desperately to find out the
secrets those factories held. All leaves were canceled in the F.B.I. G-men were on call twenty-four
hours a day.

In peacetime the F.B.I. is seldom called in until
the crime is committed. Then it goes to work to
find the criminals. In wartime this method was of
no value. If plans of important wartime weapons
were stolen and sent to Germany, the spies could
be caught but the harm could not be undone. The
job of the G-men during the war was not so much

to catch enemy agents *after* they had done their work as to prevent them from getting information.

Luckily the F.B.I. had gone to war long before the shooting began at Pearl Harbor. They had the names of thousands of members of the German-American Bund. They knew the dangerous ones, and these men were watched carefully. Loyal Americans who had been posing as members of the Bund for years kept their ears open, and when they heard anything of a suspicious nature, they immediately passed it on to the F.B.I.

Some of these persons learned of a plan to attack the Panama Canal. If the canal were destroyed, troop and supply ships from eastern ports would have to travel for weeks to reach the Pacific. G-men heard that the Germans planned to send a thousand submarines loaded with troops and explosives into the Caribbean Sea to blow up the canal. These German troops were at Dakar, in North Africa.

Fortunately, we were able to cope with this threat because of the co-operation between the various branches of our government during those dreadful war days, and because of the good relations among our allies. J. Edgar Hoover was working with the Army, Navy, and Air Force. For long hours President Roosevelt, General "Hap" Arnold of the Air Force, Admiral Ernest King of the Navy, General George Marshall of the Army, and other high-ranking officers conferred with J. Edgar Hoover.

Our Navy spread a protective net around the Caribbean Sea to guard the Panama Canal. Not a word of this ever got into the newspapers. But the German plan failed.

Meanwhile, enemy agents were being spotted and captured all over the country. In New York a woman who sold dolls for a living was arrested just as she was about to sell important naval secrets to the Japanese. In Detroit a spy was discovered in an important war plant and plans of our new planes were found in his room. A waiter on a troop ship that was about to leave for the war zone was arrested in the act of hiding a time bomb in the hold of the ship.

One of the important agents who was captured was Kurt Ludwig. The F.B.I. first heard of him in March, 1941, before Pearl Harbor. At that time a tall, middle-aged man carrying a brown brief case and accompanied by another man was knocked down and killed by a New York taxicab. People who saw the accident told police that the dead man's companion had grabbed the brief case and disappeared in the crowd.

The dead man was identified as Julio Lopez Lido, apparently a Spaniard. For some time the F.B.I. had been watching Señor Lido, but they had been unable to obtain any evidence. When they learned of the traffic accident, they investigated the dead man and found that he was not Spanish at all. He was a German whose real name was Captain Ulrich von der Osten, and he was an enemy agent.

The F.B.I. had a good description of the man who had run away with the brief case. They discovered that he was Kurt Ludwig, who had now taken Captain Osten's place as head of a spy ring.

It wasn't long before the F.B.I. picked up Ludwig's trail. They didn't arrest him—they just followed him. Ludwig went from one Army camp to another trying to get information from unsuspecting G.I.'s.

At that time we were not yet at war with Japan, and Japanese ships traveled back and forth between

West Coast ports and Tokyo. Ludwig hoped to book passage on one of these ships. He never suspected that the G-men were breathing down his neck. They grabbed him just as he was about to leave the country. After his arrest he offered one of his guards $50,000 if he would help him to escape.

When they searched his baggage they found a number of pages of blank paper. These were sent to the laboratory in Washington, where it was found that the pages had been written on in invisible ink. This was treated with chemicals, and soon the G-men found themselves with a number of pages covered with a very strange system of loops and dashes and circles.

The code experts of the F.B.I. were puzzled for a while, but finally they realized what the clever Kurt Ludwig had done. He had written many of his reports in a system of shorthand that had been invented in 1834. It had not been used for a hundred years, but the F.B.I. men soon deciphered it.

Ludwig was sentenced to twenty years in prison. Like most captured agents, he talked. Before he was finished, the F.B.I. had grabbed every member of his spy ring. Ludwig was just one of hundreds who were arrested, tried, and jailed during the war.

While the war was going on, the rest of us knew very little about the great job the F.B.I. was doing. But when the fighting came to an end, we soon realized that not one single case of sabotage had been successfully carried out in this country. We were aware, too, of the enemy's surprise when the first atomic bomb was dropped at Hiroshima. The battle on the home front had been just as important as the battle in the Pacific or in Europe, and it had been just as successful. Enemy agents had been stopped, cornered, and caught wherever they appeared. The F.B.I. really fought a great war.

11 THE POSTWAR DANGER

When World War II was over, the F.B.I. went back to its work of fighting peacetime criminals. There was a great deal of crime in the United States in the years following the war. Returning GI's had brought back thousands of pistols, carbines, and Tommy guns as souvenirs. Criminals no longer had to buy guns—they stole them from returning GI's. These guns were hard to trace, and that made the job of the F.B.I. more difficult.

In this problem the F.B.I. was taught by its scientific laboratories to use equipment that had been invented for wartime use. To locate and find hidden guns, it now employed the mine detectors that had been used by the infantry. Great advances had been made in photography and radio, too, and the F.B.I. laboratories had kept up with them. During the war the doctors had learned a great deal about blood, and doctors and chemists attached to

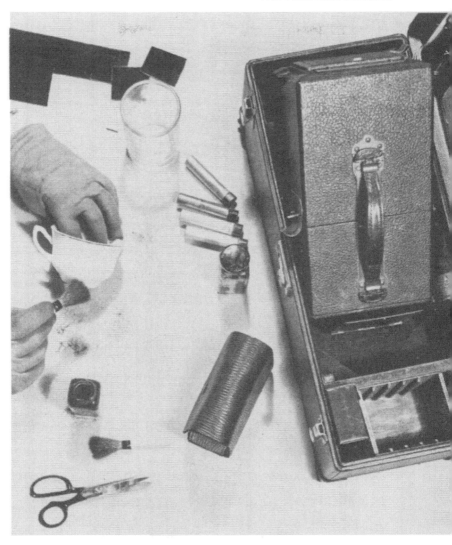

A single fingerprint expert in the F.B.I. Identification Division dusts for possible latent fingerprints. F.B.I. Identification Division, Washington, D.C.

the F.B.I. laboratories found that this information could be put to good use. New microscopes which could enlarge a speck of dust up to fifteen thousand diameters were in use in the laboratories, as was photographic equipment which could in turn enlarge the same speck of dust up to one hundred thousand diameters.

The constant war against crime in this country continued. But by 1949 we found ourselves in a new kind of war—a "cold war." Russia, which had so recently been our ally, had started a campaign of conquests similar to the one attempted by Hitler in the 1930's. But Russia was cleverer than Germany had been. Russia did not send armies marching into Czechoslovakia, Hungary, Rumania, and other countries which had been left poor by the war. Instead, she used a powerful weapon called "propaganda."

The Moscow radio poured poison into the hearts of the people of Europe. Russian agents managed to get into high offices in other governments, and gradually one country after another fell under Communist domination. Our leaders in Washington became convinced that Russia wanted to rule the world, just as Germany had once wanted to rule it. Most Americans were unaware of the danger that existed. "After all, we have the atomic bomb," people said. "That makes us the most powerful country in the world."

We did have the atomic bomb. Congress knew that the Russians would do anything to get the plans for the new type of atomic bombs our scientists were developing. In 1946 Congress had passed the Atomic Energy Act, which gave the Atomic Energy Commission the job of guarding our atomic secrets. According to this Act, any violations of the security rules which surrounded atomic research were to be investigated by the F.B.I. In addition, Congress provided that any person who was to work on the top-secret atomic bomb project must first be investigated by the F.B.I. This last item greatly increased the work of Mr. Hoover and his men, for thousands of scientists, laboratory assistants, and other employees were working on classified jobs.

The F.B.I. had to investigate every single one of these individuals. The F.B.I. did not have the job of clearing government employees. The loyalty investigation conducted by the F.B.I. merely gathered information about men who had access to ıp secrets. Then the F.B.I. turned all this information over to the heads of the various government departments. The F.B.I. did not have nor did it want to have the power to discharge any of these individuals.

J. Edgar Hoover has said publicly that he has no power to discharge anyone who does not work in his own organization. Of course, no proven Communist would continue to be employed at Oak Ridge or at Los Alamos, where atomic experiments are being carried out. He would immediately be discharged, not by Mr. Hoover but by the Atomic Energy Commission, which is in charge of all research.

When the Commission denied or revoked the security clearances of several hundred persons for access to classified material, American Communists sent up a cry that they were being persecuted. "We are a political party," their leaders shouted, "just like the Democratic or Republican parties."

J. Edgar Hoover, who probably knows more about Communism than any other living American, just smiled. He told a United States Senate committee, "The Communist Party is not a real political party. It is a highly organized, militant, and disciplined group of conspirators which follows the dictates of international Communism."

Mr. Hoover gave the committee plenty of proof that the real aim of the Communist Party is to overthrow the United States government by force, if need be. He told the committee that although there were only 25,000 active members of the Communist Party in the United States, there were thousands of Communist sympathizers and agents who were ready at all times to obey their Moscow masters.

"Would it be possible for a small group of saboteurs, well organized, to cripple a big city like New York with its eight million population?" That question was asked of Mr. Hoover by an agent who was taking his "refresher" course in Washington.

Mr. Hoover nodded solemnly and explained how a group of dedicated, well-trained saboteurs could paralyze even a big city like New York. He explained that they would have agents working in key positions in power plants, centers of communication such as the telegraph and telephone companies, and in other important key spots.

At a zero hour these saboteurs could wreck the entire power system of the city. All electricity would be cut off. Telephones, telegraphs, teletypes, and radios would be shut down. Subways would be halted in their tracks, all traffic lights in the streets would go off. The National Guard armories, well stocked with guns and ammunition and guarded by only a few men, would fall into the hands of a small organized group of Communists using Commando tactics. Within an hour these arms could be distributed to the four or five thousand men who would be waiting for them.

As soon as the men and women working in downtown offices would become aware that something serious was wrong, their only thought would be to get home to their families. The New York skyscrapers would then pour forth the millions who work in them and city-wide panic would take place.

Proof of the Communists' plans for taking over a city has been found—in the form of a dozen small paper-backed books. One bore the innocent title, "Official Regulations of the Game of Football."

An F.B.I. agent to whom the booklet was shown uttered a startled exclamation after reading the first page.

"But this has nothing to do with football!" he said. "This book explains how to destroy high-tension electrical lines, central electric plants, city reservoirs, and dozens of other important installations."

"Take a look at these other books," an older agent advised. They all looked innocent enough and all bore titles relating to various games—baseball, basketball, boxing, soccer, hockey, and softball. But the text in each book explained different ways of starting fires and of disguising the appearance of time bombs. They told how to cripple industrial plants, how to short-circuit the whole electric power of a city, and how to kill the important men in a community.

The veteran F.B.I. agent explained that all these booklets, and thousands just like them, had been discovered on a freighter. A merchant seaman aboard the ship had been told to throw a lot of damaged cargo overboard. The seaman found a box filled with sardine cans among the ruined cargo. Perhaps the sardines had not been ruined, he thought. He would open one of the cans and find out.

He took his penknife and opened one of the sardine tins. There were no sardines in the can; instead, there were thirty-three pamphlets, printed in Spanish, which appeared to be regulations for various sports.

But the only "sports" mentioned in the booklets were murder and arson and sabotage. The seaman turned over to the F.B.I. the can and its contents. The full meaning of the pamphlets then became known. They contained a complete set of sabotage methods and techniques which could destroy our country's production and war potentials.

Because of the alertness of a seaman, these pamphlets never reached the destructive people for whom they were intended. This is an example of how an ordinary citizen can cooperate with the F.B.I. and other law enforcement agencies to protect our country from its enemies.

12   THE CASE OF THE TRAITOROUS PHYSICIST

One day J. Edgar Hoover received the worst shock of his life. Even now he cannot talk about that awful moment without turning pale.

The shock came when Mr. Hoover learned that important secrets concerning the manufacture of atomic bombs had been stolen and had been delivered to Russia. For a minute he sat at his desk, completely stunned. It was hard to believe. The big atomic plants at Oak Ridge and the laboratories at Los Alamos, New Mexico, had been closely guarded.

It appeared improbable that an outsider could have slipped into either of these plants to steal the secret formulas that would reveal the newest developments in the manufacture of the atomic bomb. Yet Russia now had these secrets. Mr. Hoover had absolute proof of it lying on his desk. Where did this proof come from? Even today Mr. Hoover cannot reveal the source of this information, but there was no doubt that the information was true. Who had given these secrets to Russia?

Mr. Hoover immediately called in his top agents for a conference. When the Director of the F.B.I. has an important decision to make, he frequently calls in his assistant directors for a discussion. They are encouraged to express their views, even if these do not agree with his. After everything has been thoroughly thrashed out and every man has had his say, Mr. Hoover makes his decision.

This was perhaps the most important meeting the top G-men had ever attended. Who had given these secrets to the Russians? Every man there expressed his views. All were convinced that this had been an inside job. Every man agreed sadly that the spy must have been one of the scientists in the inner circle of atomic research. Only really great physicists and mathematicians would be able to understand the various formulas. The top G-men came to the conclusion that some scientist had turned traitor. Some scientist had made copies of the secret information and had passed it on to someone else who in turn had sent it to Russia.

On the table in front of them Mr. Hoover and his assistants had the record of every scientist working on atomic research. There were several great Italian and Swedish scientists in high positions at the atomic plants, but these were men who had come to this country many, many years before. They had all contributed their great scientific knowledge to the development of the atomic bomb. It was unthinkable that any of them could be traitors, and one by one, their names were eliminated.

This left one group of scientists still to be considered. During the war several great English physicists had come to this country to help harness the energy produced by nuclear fission for use as an atomic bomb. Mr. Hoover and his men went over the list of these men carefully. Most of them were distinguished British scientists who had been serving their country all of their lives. And all had been vouched for by the British government. One by one, they, too, were eliminated.

Then the F.B.I. agents came to the name of Dr. Klaus Fuchs. Klaus Fuchs had been born in Germany. His father had been a Lutheran minister there. When Hitler had come into power, Klaus

Fuchs had fled to England. He hated the Nazis, so it was only natural that his offer of his services should have been accepted by the British.

A truly great physicist, Fuchs quickly made a name for himself at Harwell, the site of England's atomic research plant. In 1943 he had been sent with several other British scientists to the United States to work on the atomic bomb. The British government had vouched for him, and at the time such a recommendation was enough.

He had been in the United States from 1943 to 1946. Now it was 1947 and he was back in England, holding a very important post at the Harwell plant.

Mr. Hoover told his men to find out everything they could about Fuchs from people who had known him when he was working in this country. The scientists who worked with him said that he was a shy and quiet man who had very few interests outside his work. In appearance he was tall, with slightly stooped shoulders and thinning hair. It was agreed that he seemed to be the typical dedicated scientist, interested only in his work.

Who were his friends among his scientific colleagues? He didn't have many friends, the G-men discovered. This in itself was peculiar. During the war years the scientists who were filled with such terrifying secrets became very friendly with one another. They trusted nobody but those with whom they worked. They lived together, worked together, and at night behind closed doors they would sit smoking their pipes and discussing atomic problems with one another. They seldom even saw their own families, for fear that they might let slip a careless word. They seldom associated with anyone except fellow scientists.

But Klaus Fuchs was different. When his work was done, he would leave the laboratory and no one would see him until the next morning. The F.B.I. interviewed everyone who had lived in the various apartment houses and boarding houses where Fuchs had stayed while he was in this country. Who had visited Fuchs during this time? The F.B.I. found that Fuchs occasionally had visitors late at night. They found that now and then he asked for a leave of two or three days. No one knew where he went during these absences.

Then the F.B.I. found several other clues which cannot be made public now. They are hidden in the F.B.I.'s secret files. But the clues, added to the other information, convinced J. Edgar Hoover that Klaus Fuchs was the only man who could possibly have committed what Mr. Hoover calls the Crime of the Century.

The Director of the F.B.I. immediately notified the British Secret Service what he had learned about Fuchs. They were horrified. Why, Klaus Fuchs was one of the world's greatest experts on the atomic bomb!

"That's what worries me," Mr. Hoover said sadly. "I am convinced that he has given every secret he knows to the Russians."

That was enough for MI-5. They arrested Dr. Klaus Fuchs and questioned him. Suddenly he broke down completely. He confessed that before Hitler's rise to power in Germany he had been a member of the Communist Party. Immediately after he began to work on atomic research at Harwell, he had sought out Russian agents and volunteered to give them information. He said that while he was in the United States he had furnished a great deal of top-secret material to a Russian agent. Who was the Russian agent? Fuchs said that he had no idea.

By this time Klaus Fuchs appeared horror-

stricken at what he had done. Maybe it was conscience—more likely it was fear of the death penalty. But in any case, he told the British agents everything he knew.

"What did this Russian agent look like?" MI-5 wanted to know.

"Well, he was about forty-five, and approximately five feet ten inches tall, with broad shoulders and a round face."

Where did this man live? Fuchs said he had no idea. How many times had he met him? At least a dozen times. Where? Several times in New York City, once in Boston, and twice in Santa Fe, New Mexico.

Was this man a physicist? Fuchs shook his head. He said that the man was a chemist. Was he a Russian? No, Fuchs replied. The man was obviously an American. In fact, Fuchs went on, he looked like the average American.

Some time later the confession made by Fuchs was made available to the F.B.I. Mr. Hoover and his assistants studied it in detail.

"All we know about the man mentioned by Fuchs," Mr. Hoover said sadly, "is that he is a chemist and that he looks like the average American. The last part of that description would fit at least twenty million men in this country. But," he added, "we'll get him. I don't know how, but I do know this is the greatest challenge the F.B.I. has ever been asked to meet. This man is the link between our atomic research program and Moscow. Even while we talk, he may be receiving still more secrets from other traitorous scientists and passing them on to Russia."

"How many men do you want assigned to this case, Mr. Hoover?" one of his assistants asked.

"Just as many as we need," the Director snapped. "Now let's go to work."

A special agent whom we shall call C— B— was one of those assigned to cover the Boston area. A veteran of the F.B.I., he was skillful at interviewing people, and it was for this reason that he was assigned to the Boston angle of the Klaus Fuchs case.

Klaus Fuchs had a married sister, Mrs. Kristel Heineman, who lived in Cambridge, across the river from Boston, with her husband and their two children. C— B— investigated her carefully before he went to see her. It was obvious that Mrs.

Heineman was an ordinary housewife who knew nothing at all about mathematics or physics. All the people with whom she and her husband were friendly appeared to be average Americans. She was a very religious woman—after all, her father had been a minister—and not one of her neighbors or friends was a suspicious character. C—— B—— went to see her. When he identified himself as a G-man, her face lit up.

"Are you the sister of Dr. Klaus Fuchs?" the agent asked softly.

"Yes, I am," she answered.

"Did he ever visit you when he was in this country?"

"Yes, occasionally," she replied sadly. "But he was always so busy with his work."

"Did he ever bring any friends to your house with him?"

Mrs. Heineman shook her head. "No, but a friend of his did call here at the house three times."

"What did he look like?"

"Well, he was about forty-five years old. He was stocky and had dark brown hair. I think he was a chemist."

"What makes you think that?" the agent asked.

"He had quite a way with children," Mrs. Heineman said. "My two youngsters thought he was wonderful. One time he came he brought candy for them. He asked my oldest son what he wanted for Christmas, and the boy said he wanted a chemistry set. My brother's friend was delighted at that; he said that chemistry was the most wonderful study in the world."

"Was your brother here then?"

"No, and the stranger was very disappointed. He came back a few weeks later, and this time my brother was here."

"Did they seem to know each other well?"

"Oh, yes," Mrs. Heineman replied. "They immediately went into the living room, shut the door, talked for about twenty minutes, and then the stranger left."

"By the way, what was his name?" the agent asked.

Mrs. Heineman looked blank. "It's funny," she said, "but I don't remember. I don't believe he ever mentioned his name. Perhaps my husband will know."

Just then Mr. Heineman walked into the house. He was a teacher at Harvard, and C—— B—— had investigated him thoroughly, too. He was completely above suspicion. Did Mr. Heineman know the name of the stranger?

"No," he said. "When I arrived home for lunch one day, this man was in the house. He explained that he had come here hoping to find my wife's brother, Klaus Fuchs. He was very disappointed because Fuchs wasn't here. I chatted with him awhile and asked him to stay to lunch. He was a quiet, mild-mannered sort of man, not the kind of person who would stand out in a crowd. At lunch he talked quite a lot about vitamins. I got the impression that he was either a chemist or a bacteriologist.

"Say, I just remembered something," Mr. Heineman added. "I have a vague memory that he did mumble his name when I asked him for it." He then gave C—— B—— a name which we cannot divulge. Instead, we shall use the name "James Davidson."

"He gave no hint as to where he lived, did he?" the agent asked.

"He didn't exactly say," Mr. Heineman answered, "but he mentioned Philadelphia. Maybe that's where he lives. I certainly wish I could help you more."

C— B— reported everything he had learned to F.B.I. headquarters in Washington. In the beginning this stranger had been nothing but a shadow. Now the F.B.I. knew that he was a chemist who also knew something about bacteriology. They knew that he liked children, and that he might live in Philadelphia. They knew that he had given his name as James Davidson, but they feared that the name was probably a false one.

Now the F.B.I. started the long, tedious attempt to run down this shadowy figure. There were thousands and thousands of chemists in the United States. The G-men began by getting the name of every person employed by a chemistry firm in Philadelphia and New York. When they found a chemist named James Davidson, they couldn't help but be excited. The James Davidson they found was an engineer working in New York City. He was about forty-five, brown-haired, and of stocky build. Most important, he was average looking.

G-men kept watch on Davidson twenty-four hours a day. Unknown to him, they took a great many pictures of him. Mr. Hoover put an agent on a plane with the pictures and sent him to England. The G-man and British agents went to question Fuchs, who was now in Wormwood Scrubs prison. They handed Fuchs twenty photographs, one of which was a picture of James Davidson.

"Is the man you contacted in New York, in Boston, and in Santa Fe shown here?" a British agent asked.

Doctor Fuchs studied the photographs carefully. Finally he picked up the one of James Davidson. He examined it for two minutes, looking very thoughtful. "There is something familiar about this man," he said. He then covered the forehead of the picture and added, "The man I met in the United States was usually wearing a hat. I cannot swear, but I am pretty sure that this looks like the man to whom I gave the atomic formulas."

The F.B.I. agent immediately sent a cable to Washington. Doctor Fuchs' statement was insufficient, however. There must be corroboration. The charges against Davidson were too serious for any possibility of error. The picture must be shown also to Fuchs' sister and brother-in-law.

The picture was flown to Boston. Mrs. Heineman and her husband looked at the picture blankly. "I never saw this man before in my life," Heineman said. His wife agreed.

This was a great disappointment, but the Heinemans, of course, could be wrong. It was time to bring James Davidson in for questioning. He was questioned and investigated thoroughly. He proved that he had been working in his factory on the days that Fuchs said he had met the American agent in Santa Fe and in Boston. The time card he punched at the factory proved that he could not have been anywhere but in New York City on those days. James Davidson was completely cleared.

By that time F.B.I. agents were investigating many chemists in the United States, with special attention to those working in New York and Philadelphia. Just to show what a tremendous job it was, it might be mentioned that in New York City alone there are seventy-five thousand licensed concerns where chemists could be employed. But gradually, by a process of elimination, the field of investigation began to narrow. The F.B.I. had a list of thousands of Communists in America, and the names of thousands who seemed to be Communist sympathizers. Were any of these chemists? Were any of them bacteriologists?

One name that appeared on the list of Communist sympathizers and also on the list of registered chemists was familiar to the F.B.I. The name was Abraham Brothman, a chemical engineer who owned a chemical laboratory in Long Island, New York. Brothman was known to have been associated with Communists. He had been questioned by G-men some time before, but he had insisted that his dealings with Communists had been nothing but ordinary business dealings. Others who worked in his laboratory also had been questioned at the time. One of these was a chemist named Harry Gold. There were no definite charges proven against Brothman or Harry Gold, and the case was dropped. But the names of Abraham Brothman and Harry Gold were still in the F.B.I. files.

The G-men were investigating every suspicious person, and Brothman and Gold were at least slightly suspicious persons. Brothman? He had disappeared. There remained Harry Gold, but nothing really suspicious was known about him. The story he had told when questioned was very frank and straightforward. He was just a young chemist trying to earn a living. On the other hand, he had worked for Abraham Brothman, who was a friend of known Communist agents.

The G-men decided to check up on Harry Gold, just as they had checked up on thousands of other chemists. They finally located him in Philadelphia.

13 AMERICA'S FIRST ATOM BOMB SPY

J—— S—— was one of those assigned to investigate Harry Gold. Neither he nor any of the agents who worked with him felt too hopeful at first. So many promising leads had turned out to be false. This was probably just another dead end.

The agent found that Harry Gold had been brought to the United States as a baby. His parents had fled from Russia and had come to this country to enjoy freedom of worship, freedom of speech, and the other benefits of democracy which had been denied to them in the country of their birth. They settled in Philadelphia. Young Harry went to the public schools, to the South Philadelphia High School, and then on to the University of Pennsylvania.

J—— S—— looked up the college records. He shook his head with disappointment. Harry Gold seemed to be just another normal young college student. His marks were very good—especially his marks in science. After he was graduated from college he went to work as a chemist for the Pennsylvania Sugar Company in Philadelphia. When J—— S—— went to this company to look up Harry Gold's record, he found that the young scientist had been thought of as a shy, meek, quiet man. He had been considered a good chemist who never minded working overtime so long as he could remain in his beloved laboratory.

"Harry Gold is just an average American," J—— S—— was told. "He even looks like the average man. He is not the kind of person who would ever stand out in a crowd."

The agent looked thoughtful. Where had he heard that before? Then he remembered that Mr. Heineman had used almost the same words. Still, it probably didn't mean anything.

The agent also learned that during the depression the Pennsylvania Sugar Company had been forced to lay off a great many workers. Harry Gold, being one of the newcomers, was among those dismissed, but he immediately got another job in Jersey City. His employers there also spoke highly of his work. A year later business was better, and the Pennsylvania Sugar Company rehired the bright young chemist they had been forced to dismiss. Young Harry was glad to return to Philadelphia, where his parents lived.

Harry Gold was so much interested in his work that he even attended night school at Drexel Institute in Philadelphia to get a degree in Chemical Engineering. Then, in 1938, he felt that he needed to learn even more about chemistry, so he quit work and enrolled in Xavier University in Cincinnati for a post-graduate course.

Agents in Cincinnati investigated Gold to see what they could learn about him during those days. It was the same old story. Harry Gold had been a brilliant student who had been graduated with honors. After graduation he had returned to Philadelphia and had been given an even better job at the Pennsylvania Sugar Company. He worked there all during the war. Everybody called him Harry, and everybody liked him.

After the war he was offered a very responsible position at the Philadelphia General Hospital, and he took it. He was put in charge of a specialized research project in the laboratory of the hospital. When the special agent interviewed Gold's superiors at the hospital, they said that Harry Gold was one of their most trustworthy workers.

In May, 1950, J—— S——, accompanied by another agent, went to the hospital and asked to see Gold. A few minutes later they were face to face with him, and J—— S—— had a good look at the quiet, pleasant-looking chemist. He certainly did look like the average man in the street.

"We are doing a routine check-up, Mr. Gold," J—— S—— said politely. "We have interviewed hundreds of chemists and they have cooperated very well with us."

"Anything you want, Mr. S——," Gold said. "If I can help the F.B.I., I will be only too happy to do so."

J—— S—— took a picture of Klaus Fuchs out of his pocket and flashed it in front of the chemist. "Do you know this man?" he asked.

Gold looked at the picture. "Of course," he said calmly. "That's that English atom bomb spy. I don't know him, but I certainly know who he is. His picture has been in all the papers."

"Do you mind if we take a few pictures of you, Mr. Gold?" J—— S—— asked.

"Of course not," and Gold laughed.

The agent took many pictures of the chemist, including motion pictures which would be shown to Klaus Fuchs in London. While they were being taken, J—— S—— and Harry Gold chatted on amiably. Gold talked about his work at the hospital. He told of the wonderful things being done, and of how proud he was to have had a small part in the scientific advancement the hospital was making. J—— S—— said good-bye to him and went back to Philadelphia F.B.I. headquarters.

The Special Agent in Charge of the Philadelphia office of the F.B.I. was in charge of the whole search for the suspected chemist in eastern Pennsylvania. "Any luck?" he asked J—— S——.

J—— shook his head. "No," he said. "We have pictures of him. He posed willingly. Maybe we've been barking up the wrong tree. Then again, maybe not."

"We frequently bark up a hundred wrong trees," and the Special Agent in Charge smiled, "before finding the right tree. But let's be sure this is the wrong one before we go on to another one."

When the pictures had been developed, the Special Agent in Charge told J—— S—— to fly up to Boston to show the pictures to the Heineman family. Another set of the pictures would be flown to British MI-5, which would show them to Klaus Fuchs.

J—— S—— hurried to Boston and showed the pictures to Mrs. Heineman, her husband, and the eleven-year-old son. They looked at the pictures carefully and all shook their heads.

"Is this a picture of the man who came here to see Klaus Fuchs?" the agent asked.

"No," Mr. Heineman said. "That is not the man." His wife nodded agreement.

J—— S—— went back to Philadelphia. Maybe they had been barking up the wrong tree. On the other hand, it had been five years since the Heinemans had seen the man who came to visit Klaus Fuchs. In that time, they could easily have forgotten what he really looked like.

But J—— S—— kept at it. His investigation had so far failed to show any connection between Harry Gold and Klaus Fuchs. Still, a strong element of doubt remained. Gold had in some way been associated with known Russian agents; and, more than any other suspect, he most closely fitted the description of the shadowy figure to whom Fuchs had turned over the atomic secrets.

Now a strange fact developed. A former associate of Brothman was interviewed by F.B.I. agents, and in the course of the conversation he mentioned a man named Frank Keppler as having been a friend of Brothman's. The man being interviewed stated that he had not seen Keppler for a number of years, but he felt that Keppler might be in the same line of business as Brothman—chemistry.

J—— S—— had a great number of photographs with him. He spread them on a table and asked the witness, "Do you see Frank Keppler among these pictures?"

The witness looked at them, and then without any hesitation pointed to one photograph and said, "That's Frank Keppler."

He was pointing to the picture of Harry Gold.

Why had Harry Gold ever used an alias? Why had he once used the name of Frank Keppler? Something was wrong. The needle kept swinging back to Harry Gold. Could this mild-mannered, pleasant little chemist be America's number-one traitor? Could he have been the man responsible for the crime of the century?

In company with another agent, J—— S—— went

to interview Harry Gold again. This time he went to the house where Gold lived. It was a pleasant, comfortable, two-story brick-and-stone house at 6823 Kindred Street, in the northeast section of Philadelphia.

Harry Gold greeted the agents pleasantly.

"Why did you use the alias of Frank Keppler when you were introduced to an associate of Abraham Brothman?" J—— S—— asked.

Harry Gold had an answer. He had started doing some work in the Brothman laboratories in New York while he was still employed at the Pennsylvania Sugar Company, and he didn't want his employer to know that he was contacting other chemical organizations. It was a weak alibi and he knew it.

"Have you spent much time in Boston?" he was asked.

"Never been in Boston in my life." The chemist smiled.

"Have you ever been to Santa Fe, New Mexico?"

The agent knew that if he could prove Harry Gold had been in Santa Fe during the time Klaus Fuchs worked at nearby Los Alamos, he might be able to link Gold with Fuchs. But Harry Gold denied that he had ever been to the city of Santa Fe.

"The farthest west I have ever been," Gold said, "is Cincinnati, when I went to school there. I've never been to Santa Fe."

To prove his co-operation and the fact that he had nothing to conceal, Gold offered to allow the agents to search his residence. He readily executed a written consent to search.

The agents, experienced searchers, went over his bedroom thoroughly. A pin couldn't have been hidden in that room without their finding it. When they were almost finished they had found nothing at all out of the ordinary. There remained only a bookcase to be examined, and the agents went through it carefully with Gold's help.

J— S— pulled a handful of books from the top shelf, and then he saw something which had been hidden behind them. He picked it up. It was a yellow folder marked "Santa Fe, the Capital City." In the folder, which had been issued by the Chamber of Commerce of the city, there was a detailed map of Santa Fe.

J— S— held out the folder to Harry Gold.

"You say you were never in Santa Fe?" he asked quietly.

For the first time Harry Gold's calm deserted him. His mouth twitched and his eyes blinked "Let me . . . think a moment," he gasped. Then he admitted that he was the man the agents were seeking.

Every spy makes one mistake. Harry Gold made his when he kept that particular folder.

Gold was trembling now. His hands were shaking.

"It's all over, Harry Gold," C—— B—— said. "You might as well tell us the story."

"All right, all right," Gold blurted out. "I'm the man to whom Klaus Fuchs gave the atomic secrets."

Then he told the story of the crime of the century.

Harry Gold, America's first atom bomb spy, had been leading a double life for about fifteen years. Not even his decent, hard-working parents had ever realized that their quiet, serious-minded son was a Communist agent.

The first Communist Harry Gold ever met was

a man whom we shall call Troy Niles. At first, Harry didn't know that his new acquaintance was a Communist. He told Niles how his parents had been forced to leave Russia because of persecution and because of their dreadful poverty.

"There are millions in Russia now," Troy Niles said gravely, "who are still horribly poor. If only they had the benefits of American industry, their lives would be much happier. But Russia has so little money that it can't afford to buy the secrets which make American industry so great."

"I wish I could do something to help those unfortunate people," said Harry Gold.

"You can if you want to," Troy Niles told him. "You work at the Pennsylvania Sugar Company. You know about their efficient methods. Why not give the people of Russia the secret formulas that are used by your company in refining sugar? Your employers would not be injured in any way."

That was the beginning. Gradually Harry Gold fell under the spell of Troy Niles. He gave him all the chemical formulas used by the Pennsylvania Sugar Company. Two years later Troy Niles introduced him to a friend of his whom we shall call Paul Smith.

Smith was extremely businesslike. He went straight to the point. "We're interested in solvents," he explained in clear, slightly clipped words. "There's a process involving the manufacture of absolute ethyl alcohol on which your chief chemist is working. Do you know anything about it?"

"Only in a small degree. Not much," Gold muttered.

"Look things over," Smith instructed, "and be certain not to forget about the ethyl alcohol. At our next meeting I'd like to have a written biographical sketch of yourself. Make it detailed. You are not to see Niles again. Stay away from him. If I want you to see him, I'll tell you."

So it went. The man named Paul Smith seemed to hypnotize Harry Gold. Gradually Gold began to think that he had a mission in life. His mission was to help Russia. He forgot all about the freedom and the liberty that his parents had come here to find. By 1940 Harry Gold had dedicated himself to working for Communism. He willingly accepted orders from Moscow which came to him through Paul Smith and other Soviet agents.

When he had given them all the secret formulas

owned by the Pennsylvania Sugar Company, it looked as though his usefulness were at an end. But the Communist agents were clever. They realized that Harry Gold would be a perfect messenger, or courier, because he was the kind of man who would never be noticed in a crowd. They told him of his new assignment.

Now the pattern of his life changed to meet the new demands. Harry Gold worked hard from nine to five every day, and then he was free to obey orders from his espionage bosses. Every week-end he was given some job to do. He explained his absences to his parents by saying that he had to make frequent trips out of town for his company. The old folks never suspected that anything was wrong.

During the early part of the war Gold became more and more involved in espionage work. He would travel to Rochester, to Syracuse, to New York, and to Dayton, Ohio, to pick up valuable secrets from Communists. He would deliver this information to Paul Smith.

By 1944 the Communists realized that Harry Gold had only one loyalty—to Communism and to Russia—so they decided to give him the most important job any American Communist had ever been asked to do. He was to meet the great English atomic scientist, Klaus Fuchs. He was about to commit the most traitorous act ever recorded in American history.

His instructions were these. At exactly three o'clock on a certain Saturday afternoon, Harry Gold was to go to a corner on the lower East Side of New York and stand there. He was to carry a pair of gloves in his left hand and a book with a green cover in his right hand. He was to wait until a man carrying a tennis ball in his right hand crossed the street toward him. He was to say to this man, "My name is Raymond."

Harry Gold followed orders exactly, and for the first time he met the renegade English scientist, Klaus Fuchs.

During the next six months Gold met Fuchs six or seven times in New York City. Fuchs at this time was working in New York on what the world later knew as the Manhattan Project, the development of the atom bomb. Gold and Fuchs always met at different places. Once they spent an hour strolling along the paths of Central Park. At another time they met in the Bronx.

When Fuchs had written information to pass,

he would usually advise Gold at the previous meeting. In this way, plans could be made to facilitate a rapid transfer from Fuchs to Gold to Gold's Soviet superior.

Fuchs told Gold about rumors that atomic research headquarters were to be shifted to the Southwest, probably to New Mexico. Later Gold passed on this information to his new Communist boss, who was known to him only as "John." The man "John," in turn, sent the information to Moscow. The F.B.I. afterward found out that "John" was Anatoli A. Yakovlev, who worked in the Russian Consulate.

Sometimes Fuchs would give Gold envelopes containing information. Gold merely passed them on to "John."

One day in July, 1944, Gold was ordered to meet Fuchs at the Brooklyn Museum of Art, but Fuchs did not appear. It was the first time such a thing had ever happened. Gold reported this to "John," who became alarmed. Where was Fuchs?

Gold's Soviet superior knew that Fuchs had a sister named Heineman living in Boston, so Gold was given the job of asking her where her brother could be located. In Boston, Harry Gold met Mr.

and Mrs. Heineman and their young son, who had wanted a chemistry set for Christmas.

Replying to Gold's questions, Mrs. Heineman said that her brother had been suddenly transferred. He was now stationed somewhere in the Southwest, but she was unable to say exactly where. She expected him to visit her at Christmas, which was a month away.

Gold told Mrs. Heineman that he was an old friend of Dr. Fuchs and was anxious to get in touch with him. He gave her an envelope containing a New York phone number and asked that her brother phone that number as soon as possible. It was the number belonging to Anatoli Yakovlev, who was merely known as "John."

When Mrs. Heineman asked Gold what his name was, he mumbled something that sounded like James Davidson. Gold told the F.B.I. that it was the first name that occurred to him.

A few weeks later Fuchs visited his sister in Boston, received the message that Gold had left, and phoned "John." "John" told Gold to return to Boston at once. It developed that Klaus Fuchs had important information for his fellow traitor. After saying that he was stationed at Los Alamos,

New Mexico, Fuchs gave Gold a large envelope filled with reports of the progress being made in the development of the atom bomb.

"In a few months," Fuchs said, "I expect to have some more very valuable information for you."

"Will you bring it here to Boston?" Gold asked.

"No," Fuchs said. "You forget that I am one of the most important scientists working at Los Alamos. Because of that, it was very difficult for me to get away for these few days. You will have to meet me in Santa Fe, which is not very far from Los Alamos. Meet me at three o'clock in the afternoon of the first Saturday in June. I will see you at the Castillo Street Bridge over the Santa Fe River."

Harry Gold nodded. He left the house and once again slipped into his role of the meek, quiet chemist whom no one would ever notice in a crowd.

Harry Gold traveled to Santa Fe and arrived there at 2:30 P.M. on the day appointed. He did not want to ask anyone where the Castillo Street Bridge was, for he had been taught that he was never to attract attention to himself. Instead of asking someone on the street for information, he went into the Santa Fe Museum, a building filled with exhibits about the early days of this wonderful old city. There he saw, lying on a table, a stack of yellow folders which bore on their covers the words, "Santa Fe, the Capital City."

As Harry Gold picked up one of the folders, he could not have known that the little booklet would eventually be the evidence that would send him to jail for thirty years. In the folder there was a map of Santa Fe. Gold studied it and saw that the Castillo Street Bridge was only a few minutes' walk from the museum. He hurried to the bridge, arriving just as Fuchs drove up.

Gold got into the car. A short distance out of town, they came to a stop at the side of the road. After telling Gold of the progress being made at Los Alamos, Fuchs handed him a package of information and made arrangements to meet Gold in Santa Fe on September 19.

In September Gold again met Fuchs in Santa Fe. This time the scientist handed him another package which contained valuable information regarding atomic progress.

A few days later Harry Gold was back in Philadelphia. He phoned "John" and passed on the package to him. The crime of the century had been committed. Shortly afterward Klaus Fuchs went back to England to work at the Harwell atomic plant.

Harry Gold continued to work for the Pennsylvania Sugar Company. Then he changed his job and went over to the Philadelphia General Hospital. No one in Philadelphia, not even his parents, suspected that Harry Gold was the worst traitor since Benedict Arnold.

Some months later "John" met him to announce that Stalin had awarded Gold the Order of the Red Star because of his great work in delivering the atomic secrets to Russia. "John" showed him a written order saying that he had been awarded this highest of Russian decorations.

The foregoing is the story Harry Gold told F.B.I. agents in F.B.I. headquarters at Philadelphia. Harry Gold was tried in a federal court. Just before being sentenced to thirty years in prison, he stood up and thanked the judge for having given him a fair trial. He said that the F.B.I. had treated him fairly, and that he had been well treated in prison.

"I realize now," he said bitterly, "that such a fair trial could never have happened in Russia or in any of the countries dominated by Russia. I can never express to you, Judge, nor to anyone else, how deep and horrible is the remorse I feel for my traitorous conduct."

J. Edgar Hoover personally congratulated J—— S—— for his perseverance in having kept on the trail of Harry Gold, even though Gold at first had seemed innocent. "We don't give medals to our men," Mr. Hoover said gravely.

"We don't need them, Mr. Hoover," said the agent with a smile.

14

You have just read the story of *your* F.B.I.!

This organization doesn't belong to J. Edgar Hoover. It doesn't belong to the President or to the governors of the fifty states. It belongs to everyone who is a citizen of the United States.

Six thousand G-men are working today for you and for me. They are using their excellent training to protect us from bank robbers, from kidnapers, and from enemy spies. They are risking their lives, as you read this, to keep our homes and our country safe. Today there are more than fourteen million persons in the United States with arrest records. The F.B.I. has only six thousand men to keep these lawbreakers from robbing and killing and selling out their country.

But they are six thousand well-trained men, like the agents you have been reading about.

So that the F.B.I. may keep its eyes on every

area of our country, it has divided the United States into fifty-five field divisions. An experienced G-man is in charge of each division. In one division there may be a dozen resident agencies, each a small F.B.I. headquarters. Each field division has a teletype connection to F.B.I. headquarters in Washington. The F.B.I. has built a big spider web across our land, with all its offices connected by strands of radio, teletype, telephone.

You and I hear only of the spectacular cases solved by our G-men. Every day they solve robberies, forgery cases, murders—as well as many cases which we never hear about. Sometimes when there is a trial of a criminal, a G-man who helped catch the defendant is put on the stand. When he leaves the courtroom he is often pounced on by newspaper reporters.

"Come on," one of them will ask, "tell us who tipped you off to this gang."

The F.B.I. agent will grin and say, "You know better than to ask me that question."

"Sure I do," the reporter will answer, laughing, "but you can't blame me for trying."

The F.B.I. *never* reveals the secret tips it gets from loyal citizens who have overheard or overseen something that may help to identify a lawless gang or an enemy agent. The names of the thousands who have helped the F.B.I. are buried deep in the confidential files in Washington.

I gathered all the information that is in this book from official sources, from a visit to the F.B.I. training school at Quantico, the laboratory, and from other facilities in the Washington headquarters.

You may enjoy these same privileges! If your parents ever take you to Washington, D. C., ask them to let you visit the F.B.I., which is housed in the United States Department of Justice Building. There, you will be assigned a representative to take you and your parents through the laboratories, just as I was taken through them.

Why not? "This is *your* F.B.I." Mr. Hoover has often said that himself. Mr. Hoover has gone further than that. He has said that if it weren't for you and your parents and your neighbors, the F.B.I. would not be able to operate as successfully as it does. No law enforcement agency can be effective unless it has the help of all law-abiding citizens.

How can you help? To begin with, start thinking of the officer on his beat, of the police chief in your town, of the state troopers who patrol the highways, and of the F.B.I. men as your friends. These men are among the best friends you have.

If you ever see some suspicious-looking person lurking near a neighbor's house; if you ever see a man running away from a store that has been robbed; if you ever spot the license number of an automobile that you know was stolen—in short, if you ever notice anything suspicious, tell your parents about it. They will call the police if they think the matter warrants it. The police and the F.B.I. have often been put on the right track because some bright, keen-eyed young person noticed something that looked strange and had the intelligence to report it.

During the 1962 fiscal year, 11,163 F.B.I. fugitives were located. In that 12-month period there were 12,635 convictions in F.B.I. cases, resulting in six terms of life imprisonment, and actual, suspended, and probationary sentences totaling 37,100 years, 4 months and 3 days. Of the persons brought to trial in F.B.I. cases, 96.9 per cent were found guilty. In addition, 18,921 stolen automobiles which had been transported interstate were recovered.

Meanwhile, the F.B.I. was investigating espionage activities and was doing all within its power to protect our country's internal security.

Every American, young or old, can be proud of his F.B.I.

INDEX